C000057172

Cycle TOURS

Glasgow and South West Scotland

Nick Cotton

First published in 2002 by
Philip's Ltd, a division of
Octopus Publishing Group Ltd
2-4 Heron Quays
London E14 4JP

First edition 2002
First impression 2002

Based on the original Ordnance Survey Cycle Tours series
first published by Philip's and Ordnance Survey®.

ISBN 0-540-08209-0

The route maps in this book are reproduced from
Ordnance Survey® Landranger® mapping.

Text and compilation copyright © Philip's 2002

Printed and bound in Spain by Cayfosa-Quebecor

This product includes mapping data licensed from Ordnance
Survey® with the permission of the Controller of Her Majesty's
Stationery Office. © Crown copyright 2002. All rights reserved.
Licence number 100011710

Photographic acknowledgements

AA Photo Library 10, 39, 45, 63, 93, 99, 102, 119 • EA Bowness
81 • Nick Cotton 75, 87, 109, 123 • Derek Forss 106 • Colin
Molyneux 115 • Open Space/ James Gardiner 7, 15, 21 • Judy
Todd 69 • David Williams/ David Williams Picture Library 36

Contents

Abbreviations and symbols

Directions

L	left
R	right
LH	left-hand
RH	right-hand
SA	straight ahead or straight across
T-j	T-junction, a junction where you have to give way
X-roads	crossroads, a junction where you may or may not have to give way
'Placename 2'	words in quotation marks are those that appear on signposts; the numbers indicate distance in miles unless stated otherwise

Distance and grade

The number of drink bottles indicates the grade:

🍶 Easy

🍶🍶🍶 Moderate

🍶🍶🍶🍶🍶 Strenuous

The grade is based on the amount of climbing involved.

Refreshments

Pubs and teashops on or near the route are listed. The tankard 🍺 symbols indicate pubs particularly liked by the author.

Page diagrams

The page diagrams on the introductory pages show how the map pages have been laid out, how they overlap and if any inset maps have been used.

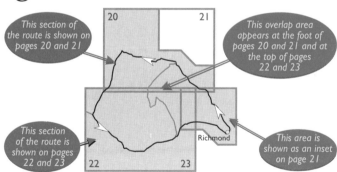

This section of the route is shown on pages 20 and 21

This overlap area appears at the foot of pages 20 and 21 and at the top of pages 22 and 23

This section of the route is shown on pages 22 and 23

This area is shown as an inset on page 21

Cross-profiles

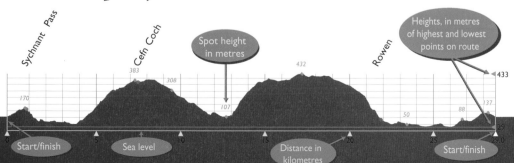

Sychnant Pass

Cefn Coch

Spot height in metres

Rowen

Heights, in metres of highest and lowest points on route

Start/finish

Sea level

Distance in kilometres

Start/finish

Legend to 1:50 000 maps

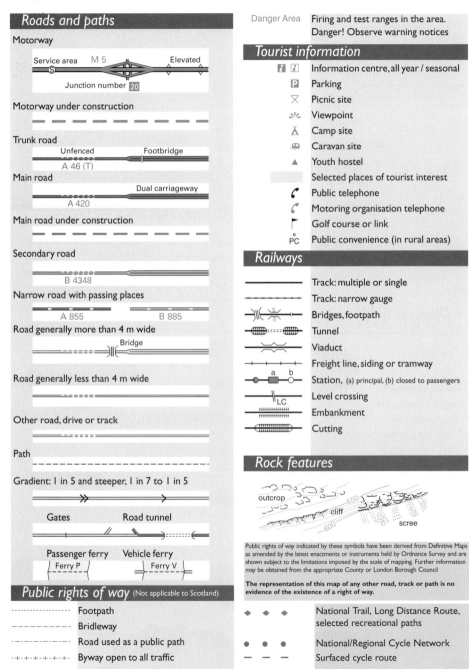

Roads and paths

Motorway

Service area M 5 Elevated
Junction number 20

Motorway under construction

Trunk road

Unfenced Footbridge
A 46 (T)

Main road

Dual carriageway
A 420

Main road under construction

Secondary road

B 4348

Narrow road with passing places

A 855 B 885

Road generally more than 4 m wide

Bridge

Road generally less than 4 m wide

Other road, drive or track

Path

Gradient: 1 in 5 and steeper, 1 in 7 to 1 in 5

Gates Road tunnel

Passenger ferry Vehicle ferry
Ferry P Ferry V

Public rights of way (Not applicable to Scotland)

·············· Footpath
– – – – – – Bridleway
–·–·–·–·– Road used as a public path
–+–+–+–+–+– Byway open to all traffic

Danger Area Firing and test ranges in the area. Danger! Observe warning notices

Tourist information

🛈 ℹ️ Information centre, all year / seasonal
🅿 Parking
✕ Picnic site
ᶰᶦᶻ Viewpoint
𝝠 Camp site
🚐 Caravan site
▲ Youth hostel
▒ Selected places of tourist interest
𝒞 Public telephone
𝒞 Motoring organisation telephone
Γ Golf course or link
PC Public convenience (in rural areas)

Railways

——— Track: multiple or single
‡‡‡‡‡ Track: narrow gauge
)||(Bridges, footpath
⬚⋯⬚ Tunnel
⌣⌣ Viaduct
+—+ Freight line, siding or tramway
●—■—○ Station, (a) principal, (b) closed to passengers
a b
—|— Level crossing
  LC
▥▥▥ Embankment
⬚⬚ Cutting

Rock features

outcrop cliff scree
—650— —600—

Public rights of way indicated by these symbols have been derived from Definitive Maps as amended by the latest enactments or instruments held by Ordnance Survey and are shown subject to the limitations imposed by the scale of mapping. Further information may be obtained from the appropriate County or London Borough Council

The representation of this map of any other road, track or path is no evidence of the existence of a right of way.

◆ ◆ ◆ National Trail, Long Distance Route, selected recreational paths

● ● ● National/Regional Cycle Network
— — — Surfaced cycle route

Water features

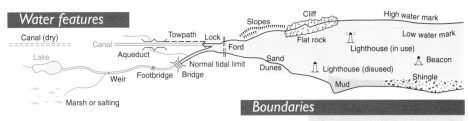

Canal (dry)
Canal
Lake
Aqueduct
Towpath
Lock
Ford
Weir
Footbridge
Bridge
Normal tidal limit
Marsh or salting

Slopes
Cliff
High water mark
Flat rock
Low water mark
Lighthouse (in use)
Sand
Dunes
Beacon
Lighthouse (disused)
Shingle
Mud

General features

ʌ̣ ʌ̣ ʌ̣	Electricity transmission line (with pylons spaced conventionally)
> - -> - ->	Pipeline (arrow indicates direction of flow)
ruin	Buildings
	Public buildings (selected)
⬭	Bus or coach station
	Coniferous wood
	Non-coniferous wood
	Mixed wood
	Orchard
	Park or ornamental grounds
	Quarry
	Spoil heap, refuse tip or dump
⊼	Radio or TV mast
▮	Church or chapel with tower
▮	Church or chapel with spire
+	Church or chapel without tower or spire
○	Chimney or tower
⌀	Glasshouse
┼	Graticule intersection at 5' intervals
Ⓗ	Heliport
△	Triangulation pillar
Ⅹ	Windmill with or without sails
Ⅰ	Windpump

Boundaries

+ — + — +	National
-o- -o- -o- -o-	London borough
	National park or forest park
NT	National Trust
— · — · —	County, region or islands area
+ + + + +	District

NT open access
NT limited access

Abbreviations

P	Post office
PH	Public house
MS	Milestone
MP	Milepost
CH	Clubhouse
PC	Public convenience (in rural areas)
TH	Town hall, guildhall or equivalent
CG	Coastguard

Antiquities

VILLA	Roman
𝕮𝖆𝖘𝖙𝖑𝖊	Non-Roman
⚔	Battlefield (with date)
☆	Tumulus
+	Position of antiquity which cannot be drawn to scale
𝔐	Ancient monuments and historic buildings in the care of the Secretaries of State for the Environment, for Scotland and for Wales and that are open to the public

Heights

— 50 —	Contours are at 10 metres vertical interval
· 144	Heights are to the nearest metre above mean sea level

Heights shown close to a triangulation pillar refer to the station height at ground level and not necessarily to the summit

A circuit of Loch Katrine from Aberfoyle

Although there are two potentially busy sections on this ride (the B829 west of Aberfoyle and the A821 over Duke's Pass), on a quiet day with good visibility, this is one of the finest on-road rides in central Scotland. There are only two real hills, both with less than a 150-m (500 ft) climb. The remote Loch Katrine is the most memorable of the lochs but the B829 runs alongside Loch Ard, Loch Chon and Loch Arklet, climbing up through forestry to over 180 m (600 ft). Views open up of the dramatic peaks to the west of Loch Lomond. You have the choice of a side trip to the west to see the banks of Loch Lomond and the only chance of refreshments (at Inversnaid) until the east end of Loch Katrine. The latter, along with so much of the region, is Rob Roy country and there are many signposts around the loch with details of local history. A final loch (Loch Achray) is visited before the last and steepest climb of the day over Duke's Pass.

Start

The Forth Inn, Aberfoyle, 40 km (25 miles) north of Glasgow on the A81

P Follow signs

Distance and grade

51 km (32 miles) with a further 11 km (7 mile) side trip

/// Moderate

Terrain

Several lochs; forestry; open hillsides and views of mountains. Total height gain – 740 m (2425 ft)

Nearest railway

Milngavie, 16 km (10 miles) south of the route at Killearn (instruction 11)

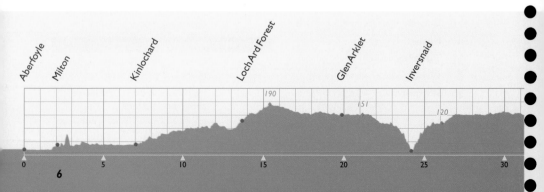

Aberfoyle Milton Kinlochard Loch Ard Forest Glen Arklet Inversnaid

190 151 120

0 5 10 15 20 25 30

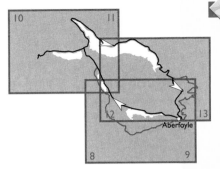

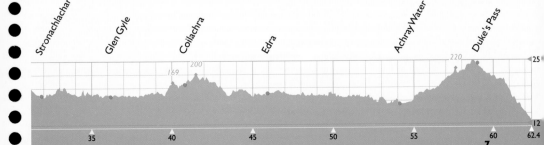
Inversnaid 3

Views from above the Snaid Burn ravine take in the 'Arrochar Alps' and the narrows of Loch Lomond. From the waterfall above the tiny harbour, a footbridge leads south along the West Highland Way, beside the loch. Loch Lomond is the largest loch in Scotland – 37 km (23 miles) long, up to 8 km (5 miles) wide, and 190 m (630 ft) deep at the deepest point

Loch Katrine 4/6

A reservoir in the Trossachs, surrounded by woodland. There are a series of signboards around the loch with historical details of the area that are well worth stopping to read. The Visitor Centre at Trossachs is the departure point for rides in the turn-of-the-century steamer

Portnellan 5

Loch Katrine was at the heart of Clan Gregor territory. The clan was established in Glen Gyle around 1533 and later expanded into Balquhidder, Glenorchy, Breadalbane and Rannoch. Portnellan is the historic burial ground. The inscription over the gateway bears the MacGregor crest

▲ *Loch Ard with Ben Lomond*

Refreshments

*Plenty of choice in **Aberfoyle** Inversnaid Hotel, **Inversnaid** Captain's Rest Cafe, at the east end of **Loch Katrine***

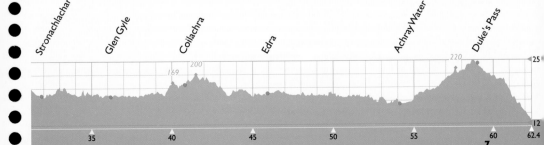

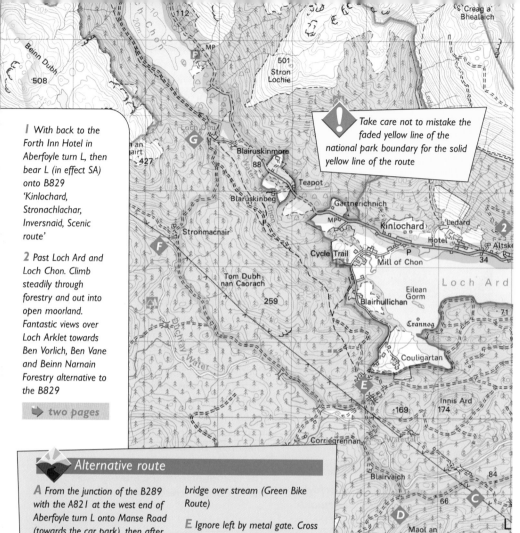

1 With back to the Forth Inn Hotel in Aberfoyle turn L, then bear L (in effect SA) onto B829 'Kinlochard, Stronachlachar, Inversnaid, Scenic route'

2 Past Loch Ard and Loch Chon. Climb steadily through forestry and out into open moorland. Fantastic views over Loch Arklet towards Ben Vorlich, Ben Vane and Beinn Narnain Forestry alternative to the B829

➡ **two pages**

Take care not to mistake the faded yellow line of the national park boundary for the solid yellow line of the route

Alternative route

A From the junction of the B289 with the A821 at the west end of Aberfoyle turn L onto Manse Road (towards the car park), then after 300 m (yd) 1st tarmac road to the R 'Covenanters Inn, Blue Bike Route'

B After 4 km (2½ miles) at junction of tracks by sign with 'Private property,. Dogs bite' bear L

C Cross two bridges. Gently uphill alongside telegraph poles. At T-j R downhill towards pylons and bridge, then bear L (i.e. do not cross bridge)

D **Easy to miss.** After 1 km (¾ mile) 1st R over small concrete bridge over stream (Green Bike Route)

E Ignore left by metal gate. Cross bridge over river, pass beneath power lines. At T-j with old railway bridge to the right turn L

F Ignore several left turns over next 5 km (3 miles). Pass beneath power lines and climb. At T-j R 'Red Route' ('Comer' is signed to the left)

G Track joins from the right by second 'Comer' sign. At fork at the bottom of a dip by buildings bear L steeply uphill

➡ **two pages**

11 The Green Bike Route climbs steeply, then descends over 3 km (2 miles). As views over Aberfoyle and golf course open up to the right turn sharp R downhill towards buildings. At T-j with A821 in Aberfoyle turn R

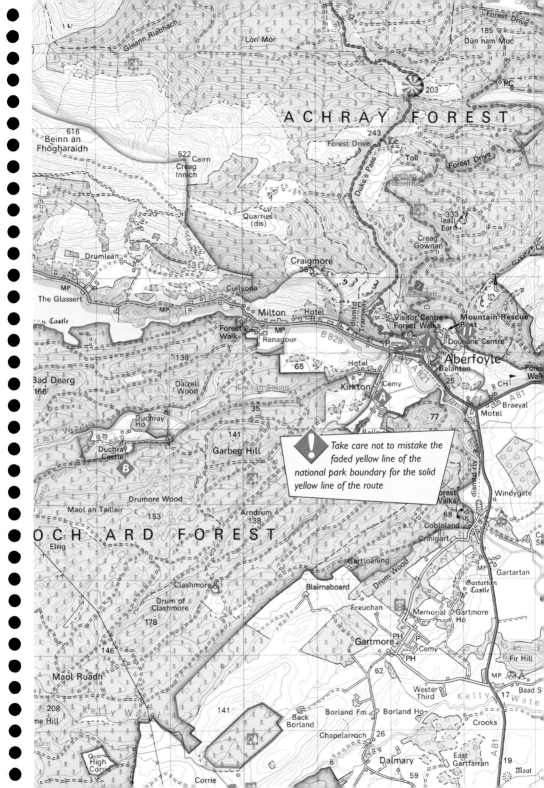

Take care not to mistake the faded yellow line of the national park boundary for the solid yellow line of the route

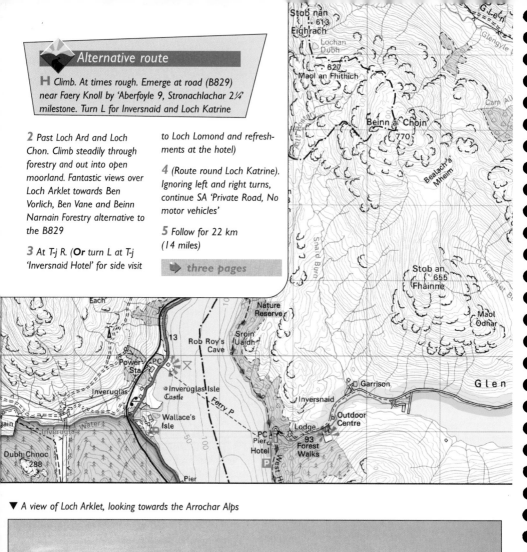

Alternative route

H Climb. At times rough. Emerge at road (B829) near Faery Knoll by 'Aberfoyle 9, Stronachlachar 2¼' milestone. Turn L for Inversnaid and Loch Katrine

2 Past Loch Ard and Loch Chon. Climb steadily through forestry and out into open moorland. Fantastic views over Loch Arklet towards Ben Vorlich, Ben Vane and Beinn Narnain Forestry alternative to the B829

3 At T-j R. (**Or** turn L at T-j 'Inversnaid Hotel' for side visit to Loch Lomond and refreshments at the hotel)

4 (Route round Loch Katrine). Ignoring left and right turns, continue SA 'Private Road, No motor vehicles'

5 Follow for 22 km (14 miles)

➡ three pages

▼ A view of Loch Arklet, looking towards the Arrochar Alps

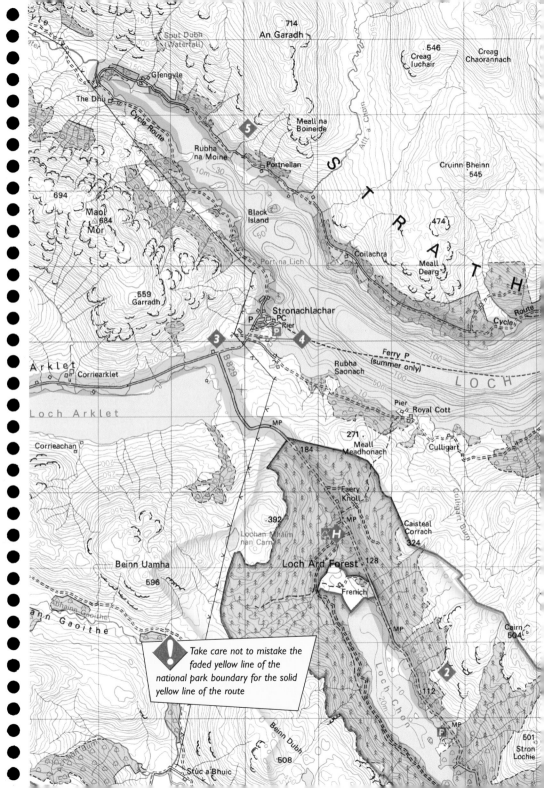

Take care not to mistake the
faded yellow line of the
national park boundary for the solid
yellow line of the route

Take care not to mistake the faded yellow line of the national park boundary for the solid yellow line of the route

5 Follow for 22 km (14 miles)

6 Through the car parking area by the steamboat quay. At T-j with A821 R. Follow this road for 10 km (6 miles) to Aberfoyle, back to the start. (**Or** to avoid the main road, busy in summer, see below for off-road alternative)

7 (Forestry route to Aberfoyle). Follow the A821 towards Aberfoyle, crossing river and passing hotel to the right. Shortly after 2 storey cottage on the right, at the start of the climb, take the 1st track to the L by wooden barrier and stone wall 'Red Bike Route'

8 At T-j with Forest Drive bear L on the Green Bike Route

9 To visit the Byre Inn in Brig o' Turk go past the loch and over cattle grid. As the Forest Drive swings right bear L towards stone farm and barn. Go through gate/over stile 'Byre Inn' and follow this track past the farm on the left, over bridge to the inn

10 Follow the Green Bike Route as it climbs, then descends to Loch Drunkie

11 The Green Bike Route climbs steeply, then descends over 3 km (2 miles). As views over Aberfoyle and golf course open up to the right turn sharp R downhill towards buildings. At T-j with A821 in Aberfoyle turn R to return to the start

Beneath the Campsie Fells, south of Aberfoyle

The beginning and end sections of this route carry significant quantities of traffic on summer weekends and you should plan accordingly: start early in the morning or try to do the ride on a weekday or out of the high season. The ride follows the A81 east from Aberfoyle past woodland and pastures and the charming Lake of Menteith. Ahead lie the dramatic cliffs of the Gargunnock and Fintry Hills while behind there are ever better views of the Trossachs. A quiet lane beneath the Campsie Fells is followed west to Balfron. The attractive villages of Killearn and Drymen are both full of pubs and other refreshment stops before the major climb of the day up through Garadhban Forest to the high point of the ride at 220 m (720 ft). The long, fast and straight descent to cross Kelty Water is followed by the last climb of the day up through Gartmore. Should you be on a hybrid or mountain bike you can work out a route through Loch Ard Forest back to Aberfoyle to avoid the last busy 3 km (2 mile) section.

Start

The Forth Inn, Aberfoyle, 40 km (25 miles) north of Glasgow on the A81

P Follow signs

Distance and grade

56 km (35 miles)

Moderate

Terrain

Loch views; broadleaf woodland and views of the Trossachs. Total height gain – 690 m (2265 ft)

Nearest railway

Milngavie, 16 km (10 miles) south of the route at Killearn (instruction 11)

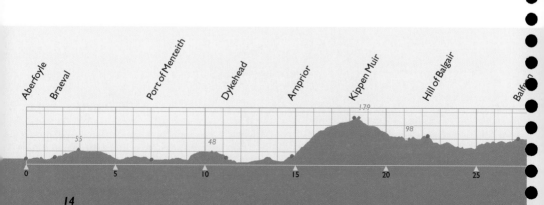

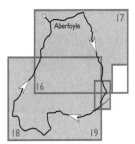

Aberfoyle

17

16

18   19

Refreshments

Plenty of choice in **Aberfoyle**
Old Mill Inn, Black Bull PH,
coffee shop, **Killearn**
Clachan PH , Winnock PH ,
plenty of choice in **Drymen**

Places of interest

Pots of Gartness 12/13

These rocky falls on the River Endrick
are renowned as a 'leap' during the
autumn run of salmon. Downstream,
only the site remains of Gartness Castle,
where the great mathematician John
Napier often worked. He is usually cred-
ited with having invented logarithms
(and the word itself)

Drymen 14

This charming village, centred around an
attractive village square, is the gateway
to the eastern shores of Loch Lomond.
The name derives from the Celtic word
'ridge' or 'knoll', describing the landscape
around the village

▼ Buchanan Castle

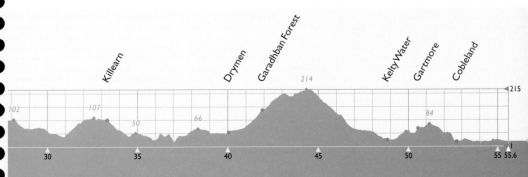

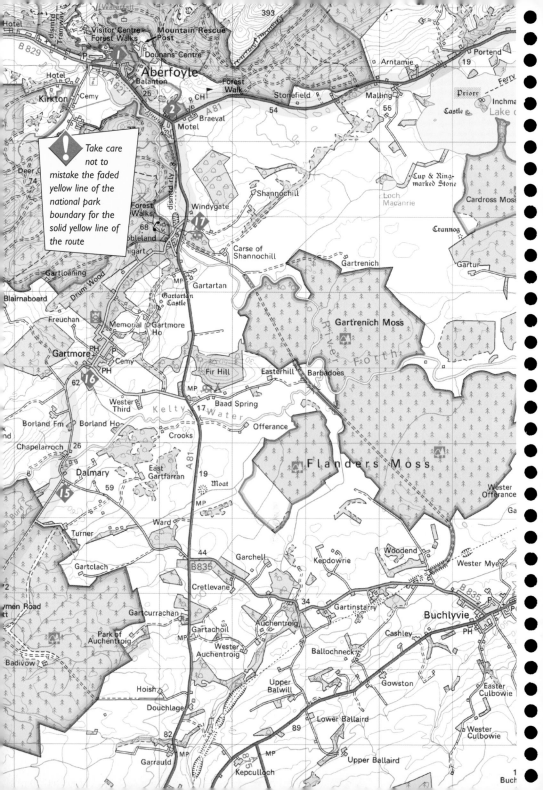

Take care not to mistake the faded yellow line of the national park boundary for the solid yellow line of the route

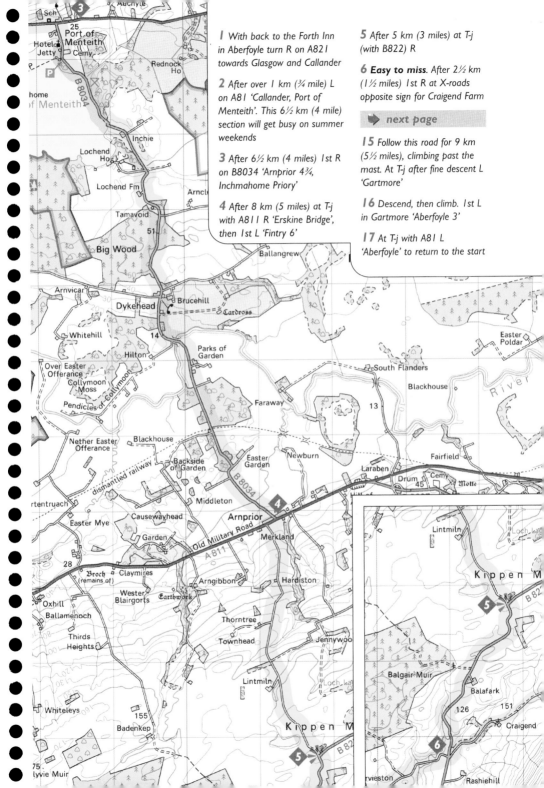

1 With back to the Forth Inn in Aberfoyle turn R on A821 towards Glasgow and Callander

2 After over 1 km (¾ mile) L on A81 'Callander, Port of Menteith'. This 6½ km (4 mile) section will get busy on summer weekends

3 After 6½ km (4 miles) 1st R on B8034 'Arnprior 4¾, Inchmahome Priory'

4 After 8 km (5 miles) at T-j with A811 R 'Erskine Bridge', then 1st L 'Fintry 6'

5 After 5 km (3 miles) at T-j (with B822) R

6 **Easy to miss**. After 2½ km (1½ miles) 1st R at X-roads opposite sign for Craigend Farm

➡ **next page**

15 Follow this road for 9 km (5½ miles), climbing past the mast. At T-j after fine descent L 'Gartmore'

16 Descend, then climb. 1st L in Gartmore 'Aberfoyle 3'

17 At T-j with A81 L 'Aberfoyle' to return to the start

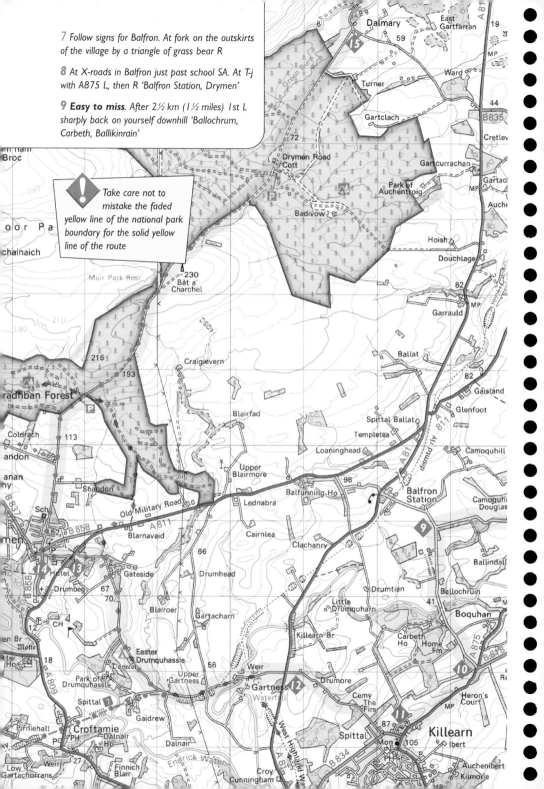

7 Follow signs for Balfron. At fork on the outskirts of the village by a triangle of grass bear R

8 At X-roads in Balfron just past school SA. At T-j with A875 L, then R 'Balfron Station, Drymen'

9 **Easy to miss**. After 2½ km (1½ miles) 1st L sharply back on yourself downhill 'Ballochrum, Carbeth, Ballikinrain'

! Take care not to mistake the faded yellow line of the national park boundary for the solid yellow line of the route

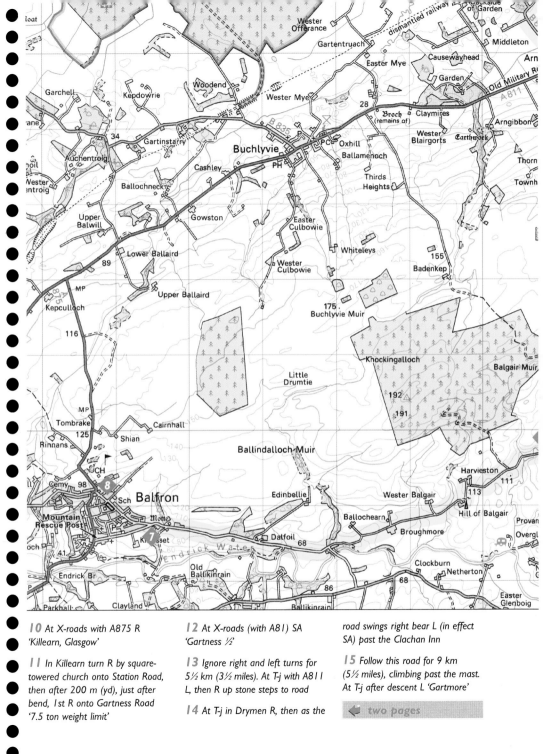

10 At X-roads with A875 R 'Killearn, Glasgow'

11 In Killearn turn R by square-towered church onto Station Road, then after 200 m (yd), just after bend, 1st R onto Gartness Road '7.5 ton weight limit'

12 At X-roads (with A81) SA 'Gartness ½'

13 Ignore right and left turns for 5½ km (3½ miles). At T-j with A811 L, then R up stone steps to road

14 At T-j in Drymen R, then as the road swings right bear L (in effect SA) past the Clachan Inn

15 Follow this road for 9 km (5½ miles), climbing past the mast. At T-j after descent L 'Gartmore'

◄ two pages

3 *The Gargunnock and Fintry Hills, west of Stirling*

Stirling is rightly famed for its magnificent castle and it is well worth at least strolling through the old town, around the castle walls. The A811 to the west of Stirling is a very busy road and unfortunately must be faced for two short sections, each of about 2½ km (1½ miles). There is an off-road alternative to the second section from the west end of Gargunnock to join the minor lane south of the A811. With the parallel B822 taking all the traffic, this gated road is heaven for cyclists: a steady climb alongside Boquhan Burn beneath the dramatic cliffs of the Gargunnock and Fintry Hills. Fintry is your last chance of refreshment before the climb past Carron Valley Reservoir to the high point of the ride at 350 m (1150 ft) on top of Earl's Hill. This is followed by a descent over 8 km (5 miles). One final, short climb after crossing the famous Bannock Burn takes you through woodland to the outskirts of Stirling.

Start

The clocktower/ George Christie Monument on Port Street/Kings Park Road in the centre of Stirling

P Follow signs

Distance and grade

50 km (31 miles)

Moderate/strenuous

Terrain

Valley of the River Forth; pasture and moorland rising to 350 m (1150 ft). Total height gain – 700 m (2300 ft)

Nearest railway

Stirling

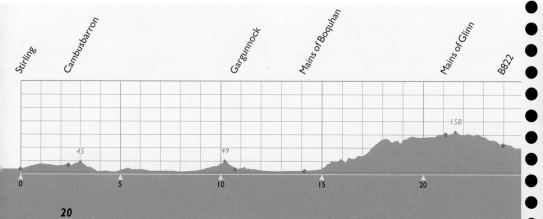

▼ *Stirling Castle*

Stirling 1

The castle stands on a rock 76 m (250 ft) high and most of the main buildings date from the 15th and 16th centuries. The Church of the Holy Rude dates from 1414. The monument commemorating Sir William Wallace's 1297 victory over the English was erected in the 19th century. The Smith Art Gallery and Museum has a programme of exhibitions on art, history, craft and design

Bannockburn 3 km (2 miles) southeast of Stirling 1

Site of the 1314 battle when Robert Bruce's army secured Scottish independence by defeating Edward II's forces. The battle is commemorated at Bannock Heritage Centre, on the site of Bruce's headquarters

Fintry 9

'Oot of the world and into Fintry' used to be the catch-phrase for this strung-out village in the Endrick Valley that still has an air of ancient remoteness. Locked between the Fintry Hills and the Campsie Fells, its business is hill grazing and has been since the 13th century. Five kilometres (3 miles) east of the village is the Loup of Fintry – a ribbon of white water plunging 27 m (90 ft) from a rocky ledge

Refreshments

Settle PH 🍷, plenty of choice in **Stirling**
Gargunnock Inn, **Gargunnock**
The Clachan PH, Fintry Inn, Coffee Pot, **Fintry**

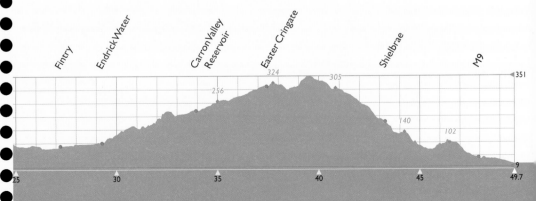

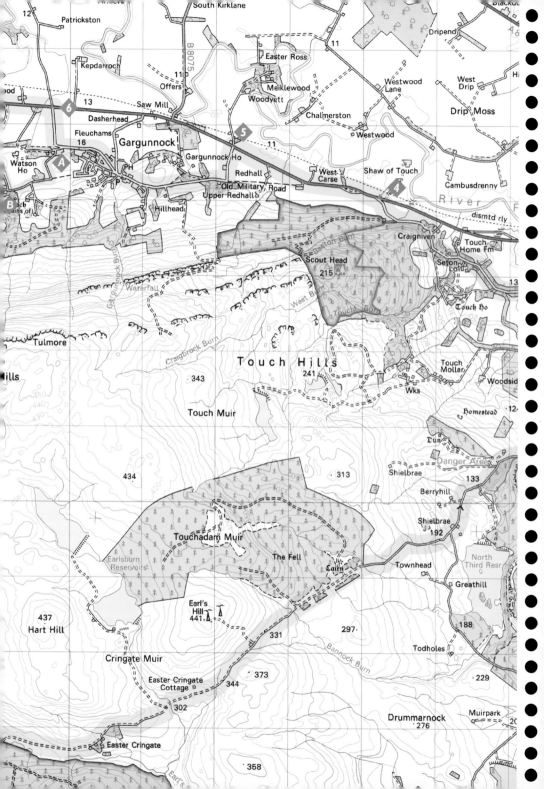

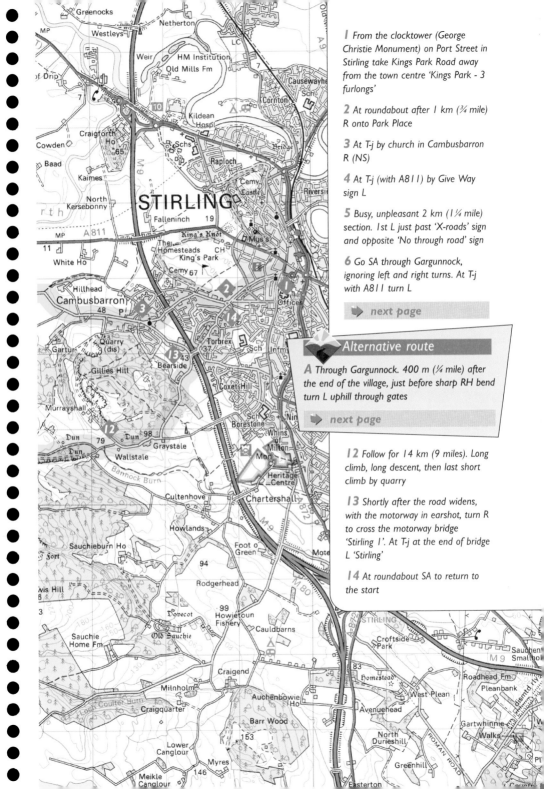

1 From the clocktower (George Christie Monument) on Port Street in Stirling take Kings Park Road away from the town centre 'Kings Park - 3 furlongs'

2 At roundabout after 1 km (¾ mile) R onto Park Place

3 At T-j by church in Cambusbarron R (NS)

4 At T-j (with A811) by Give Way sign L

5 Busy, unpleasant 2 km (1¼ mile) section. 1st L just past 'X-roads' sign and opposite 'No through road' sign

6 Go SA through Gargunnock, ignoring left and right turns. At T-j with A811 turn L

➡ next page

Alternative route

A Through Gargunnock. 400 m (¼ mile) after the end of the village, just before sharp RH bend turn L uphill through gates

➡ next page

12 Follow for 14 km (9 miles). Long climb, long descent, then last short climb by quarry

13 Shortly after the road widens, with the motorway in earshot, turn R to cross the motorway bridge 'Stirling 1'. At T-j at the end of bridge L 'Stirling'

14 At roundabout SA to return to the start

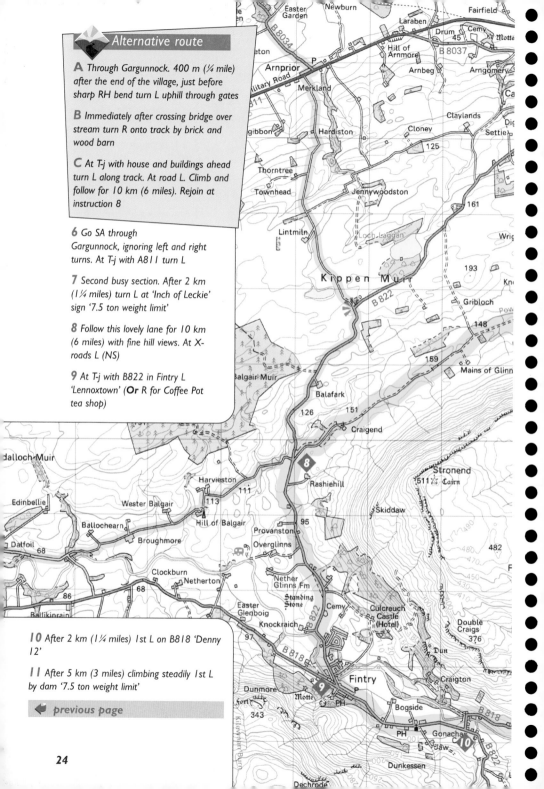

Alternative route

A Through Gargunnock. 400 m (¼ mile) after the end of the village, just before sharp RH bend turn L uphill through gates

B Immediately after crossing bridge over stream turn R onto track by brick and wood barn

C At T-j with house and buildings ahead turn L along track. At road L. Climb and follow for 10 km (6 miles). Rejoin at instruction 8

6 Go SA through Gargunnock, ignoring left and right turns. At T-j with A811 turn L

7 Second busy section. After 2 km (1¼ miles) turn L at 'Inch of Leckie' sign '7.5 ton weight limit'

8 Follow this lovely lane for 10 km (6 miles) with fine hill views. At X-roads L (NS)

9 At T-j with B822 in Fintry L 'Lennoxtown' (**Or R** for Coffee Pot tea shop)

10 After 2 km (1¼ miles) 1st L on B818 'Denny 12'

11 After 5 km (3 miles) climbing steadily 1st L by dam '7.5 ton weight limit'

◀ previous page

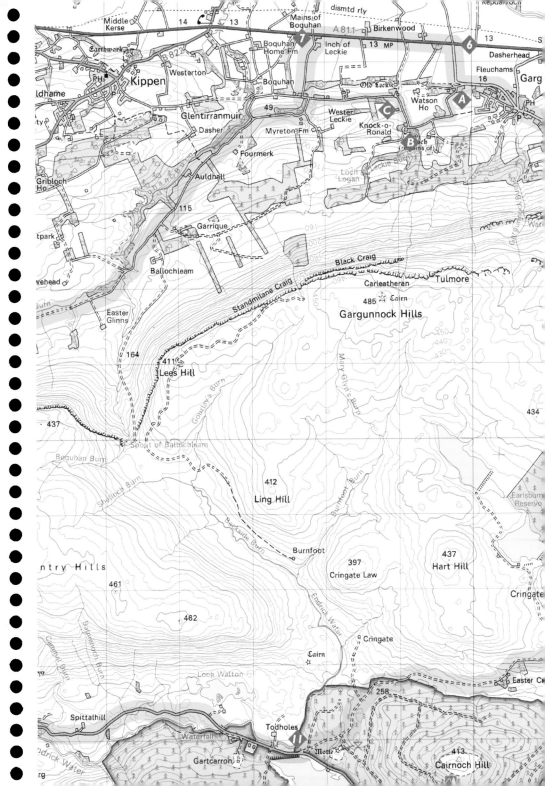

In and out of the valleys between Strathaven and Lanark

Start

Common Green (the main square), Strathaven, southeast of Glasgow

P Follow signs

Distance

58 km (36 miles). Short route (excludes Lanark) 46 km (29 miles)

Strenuous

Moderate on short route

Strathaven is a small, pleasant town with a wide central square. The bridge across Avon Water, close to the old railway viaduct, is one of the highlights of the outward route, as are the glimpses of Craignethan Castle on the drop into, and the steep climb out of, the Nethan Valley. You have two options in this ride. You can go for the short option and turn south to Lesmahagow; however, if you are feeling strong, Lanark beckons with two further steep climbs to negotiate – both out of the Clyde Valley. The approach to Lanark uses an old county road parallel with the A72 and takes you up into the heart of the town. South from Lanark, the distinctive shape of Tinto, rising to 710 m (2320 ft), looms to your left. The short and long routes rejoin near to

Refreshments

Plenty of choice in **Strathaven**
Plenty of choice in **Lanark**
Plenty of choice in **Lesmahagow**

Lesmahagow and the second crossing of the River Nethan.

Enjoy the quiet delights of the lane leading west from Lesmahagow as the final stretch on the B7086 may carry a reasonable volume of traffic (3–4 cars per minute).

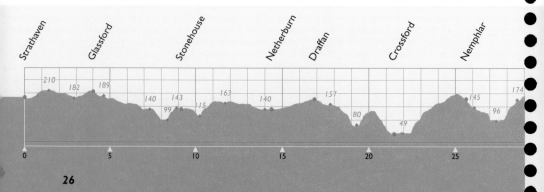

Rolling hills, steep wooded valleys either side of the Rivers Nethan and Clyde. Total height gain – 1050 m (3445 ft) or 610 m (2000 ft) on short route

Nearest railway

Lanark

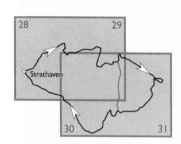

Places of interest

Stonehouse 5

The village developed from the mid-18th century, primarily due to weaving. With industrialisation, the coal mining became prominent, prospering in the parish until its demise in 1958, when Canderigg Colliery finally closed

Craignethan Castle 12

Fine example of 16th-century military architecture in a picturesque setting above the small River Nethan. It was the stronghold of the Hamiltons, supporters of Mary, Queen of Scots, and was partly dismantled by her opponents in 1579

Lanark 19

Peaceful market town, declared a royal burgh when David I built a castle in the 12th century, now vanished. The popular hero William Wallace is said to have lived and raised his forces here for Wars of Independence. His statue stands in the 1777 parish church

Corra Linn New Lanark 19

The restored cotton-milling village of New Lanark is the access point to a spectacular Scottish Wildlife Trust reserve, and has footpaths on both wooded banks of the precipitous rock-walled gorge. First of the falls up-river is Corra Linn. In 1708, a 'hall of mirrors' was built where visitors would seem to be entirely surrounded by water. Although it is usually diverted to a power station, four days a year the full force of the River Cylde is released into its natural channel, a spectacle which delighted Turner, Wordsworth, Coleridge and Scott

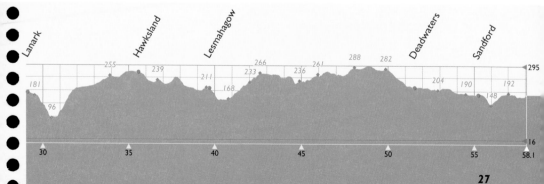

1 From traffic lights at the end of the square (Common Green) in Strathaven R onto Green Street

2 Cross bridge, go past church. At next traffic lights R on the A723 'Hamilton, Motherwell'. Follow signs for Glassford

3 At T-j at the end of Millar Street in Glassford L, then R at mini round-about onto Jackson Street 'Stonehouse 3'

4 At T-j R 'Stonehouse 1¼'

5 Downhill, cross bridge, climb steeply. At X-roads in Stonehouse at the end of Trongate L

6 **Easy to miss**. At the end of town R downhill onto Candermill Road

7 At X-roads (with B7078) by 'Stop' sign SA across bridge over M74, then 1st R (NS)

8 Follow the road L, then R past farm. At T-j at the bottom of the hill R 'Broomfield Road' and follow road round sharp LH bend

9 Follow road through Netherburn. At T-j bear R

10 After 2½ km (1½ miles) 1st L 'Craignethan Castle'

11 At T-j L 'Craignethan Castle'

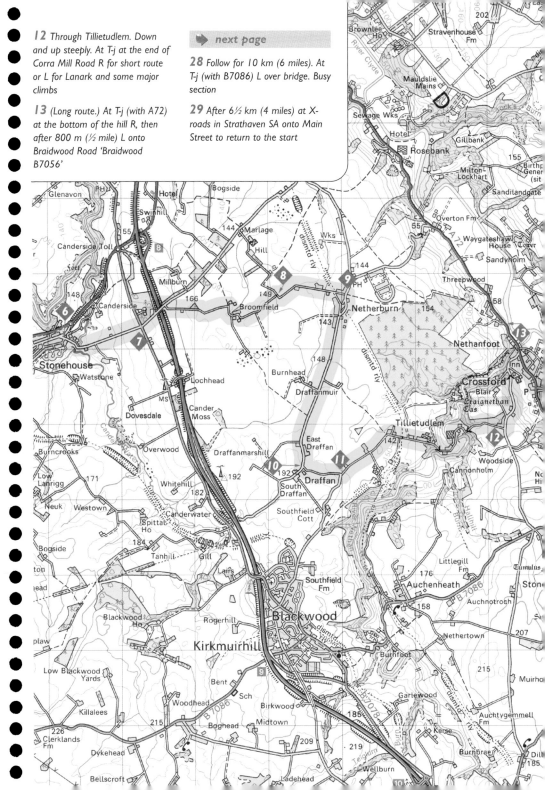

12 *Through Tillietudlem. Down and up steeply. At T-j at the end of Corra Mill Road R for short route or L for Lanark and some major climbs*

13 *(Long route.) At T-j (with A72) at the bottom of the hill R, then after 800 m (½ mile) L onto Braidwood Road 'Braidwood B7056'*

➡ **next page**

28 *Follow for 10 km (6 miles). At T-j (with B7086) L over bridge. Busy section*

29 *After 6½ km (4 miles) at X-roads in Strathaven SA onto Main Street to return to the start*

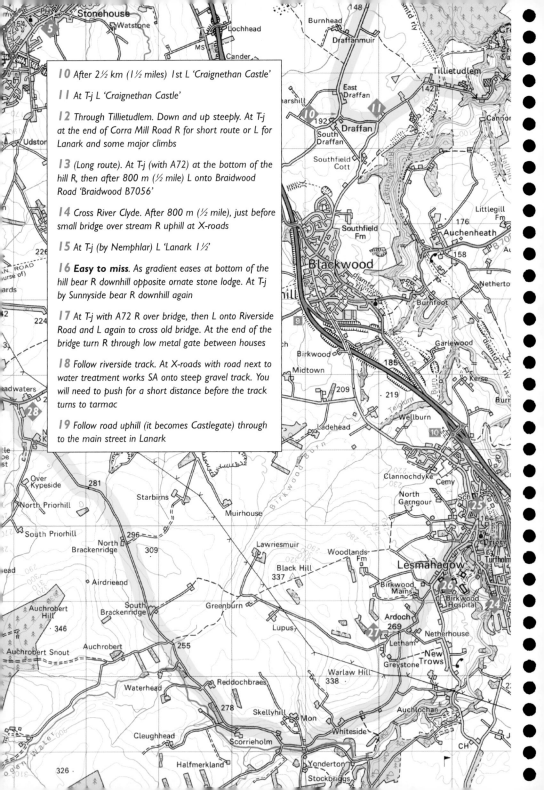

10 After 2½ km (1½ miles) 1st L 'Craignethan Castle'

11 At T-j L 'Craignethan Castle'

12 Through Tillietudlem. Down and up steeply. At T-j at the end of Corra Mill Road R for short route or L for Lanark and some major climbs

13 (Long route). At T-j (with A72) at the bottom of the hill R, then after 800 m (½ mile) L onto Braidwood Road 'Braidwood B7056'

14 Cross River Clyde. After 800 m (½ mile), just before small bridge over stream R uphill at X-roads

15 At T-j (by Nemphlar) L 'Lanark 1½'

16 **Easy to miss**. As gradient eases at bottom of the hill bear R downhill opposite ornate stone lodge. At T-j by Sunnyside bear R downhill again

17 At T-j with A72 R over bridge, then L onto Riverside Road and L again to cross old bridge. At the end of the bridge turn R through low metal gate between houses

18 Follow riverside track. At X-roads with road next to water treatment works SA onto steep gravel track. You will need to push for a short distance before the track turns to tarmac

19 Follow road uphill (it becomes Castlegate) through to the main street in Lanark

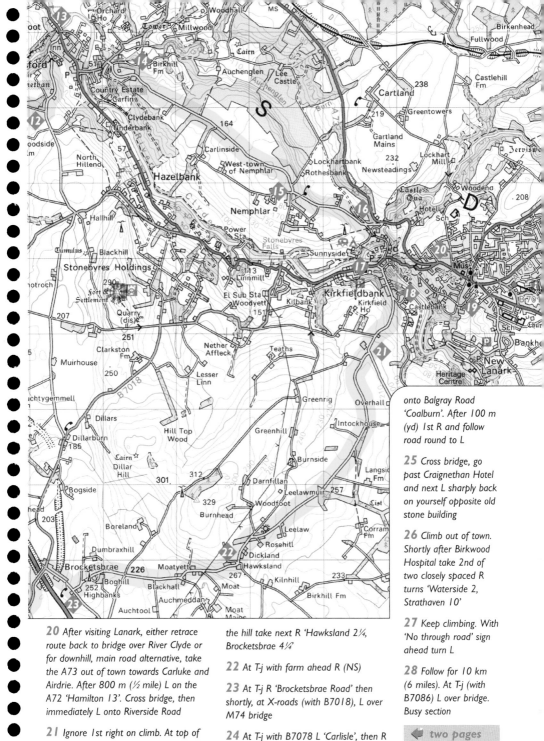

20 After visiting Lanark, either retrace route back to bridge over River Clyde or for downhill, main road alternative, take the A73 out of town towards Carluke and Airdrie. After 800 m (½ mile) L on the A72 'Hamilton 13'. Cross bridge, then immediately L onto Riverside Road

21 Ignore 1st right on climb. At top of the hill take next R 'Hawksland 2¼, Brocketsbrae 4¼'

22 At T-j with farm ahead R (NS)

23 At T-j R 'Brocketsbrae Road' then shortly, at X-roads (with B7018), L over M74 bridge

24 At T-j with B7078 L 'Carlisle', then R onto Balgray Road 'Coalburn'. After 100 m (yd) 1st R and follow road round to L

25 Cross bridge, go past Craignethan Hotel and next L sharply back on yourself opposite old stone building

26 Climb out of town. Shortly after Birkwood Hospital take 2nd of two closely spaced R turns 'Waterside 2, Strathaven 10'

27 Keep climbing. With 'No through road' sign ahead turn L

28 Follow for 10 km (6 miles). At T-j (with B7086) L over bridge. Busy section

two pages

5 *Big open country-side, west from Strathaven*

This ride from Strathaven ventures into this big, open country of forestry, moorland, sheep-grazing and outlying stone-built farmhouses. The ride heads southwest, parallel with Avon Water, whose source lies on the flanks of the Blackside. Two short, unpleasant stretches of the A71 cannot be avoided. After this, the most traffic you are likely to see is in the one pub village of Sorn some way to the south. The climb away from the A71 is rewarded with some fine views west towards the dramatic island of Arran. The directions could almost be 'keep turning left for many kilometres until rejoining the outward route' as there are no roads across the expanse of marginal farmland and moorland. Sorn is the only chance of refreshment on the ride, after which the route undulates as it crosses the valleys of the River Ayr and Greenock Water. After passing Glengavel Reservoir, the outward route is rejoined back to the start.

Start

Common Green (the main square) in Strathaven, southeast of Glasgow

P Follow signs

Distance and grade

70 km (44 miles)

Strenuous

Terrain

In and out of the three valleys formed by Avon Water and the Rivers Irvine and Ayr. Remote moorland and high pastureland southwest of Strathaven. Total height gain – 800 m (2625 ft)

Refreshments

Plenty of choice in **Strathaven**
Sorn Inn, **Sorn**

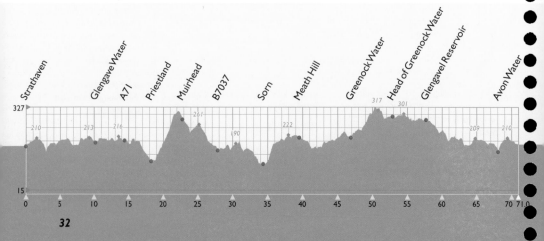

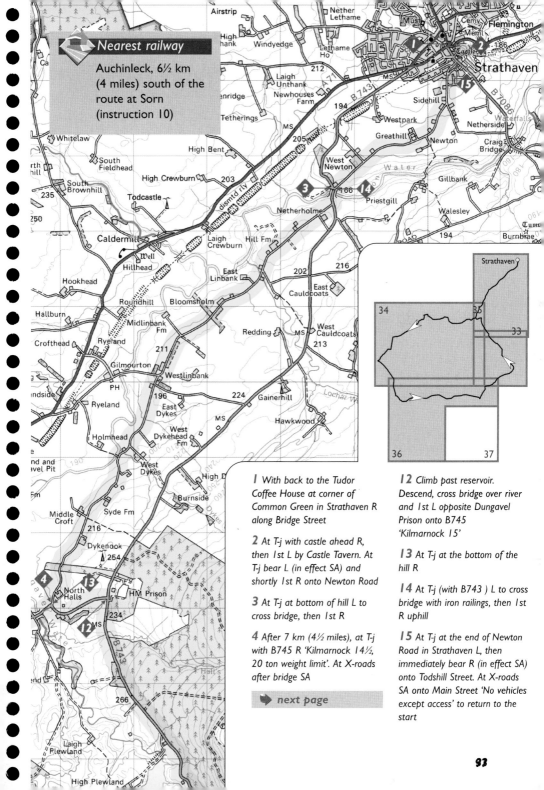

Nearest railway

Auchinleck, 6½ km (4 miles) south of the route at Sorn (instruction 10)

1 With back to the Tudor Coffee House at corner of Common Green in Strathaven R along Bridge Street

2 At T-j with castle ahead R, then 1st L by Castle Tavern. At T-j bear L (in effect SA) and shortly 1st R onto Newton Road

3 At T-j at bottom of hill L to cross bridge, then 1st R

4 After 7 km (4½ miles), at T-j with B745 R 'Kilmarnock 14½, 20 ton weight limit'. At X-roads after bridge SA

➡ next page

12 Climb past reservoir. Descend, cross bridge over river and 1st L opposite Dungavel Prison onto B745 'Kilmarnock 15'

13 At T-j at the bottom of the hill R

14 At T-j (with B743) L to cross bridge with iron railings, then 1st R uphill

15 At T-j at the end of Newton Road in Strathaven L, then immediately bear R (in effect SA) onto Todshill Street. At X-roads SA onto Main Street 'No vehicles except access' to return to the start

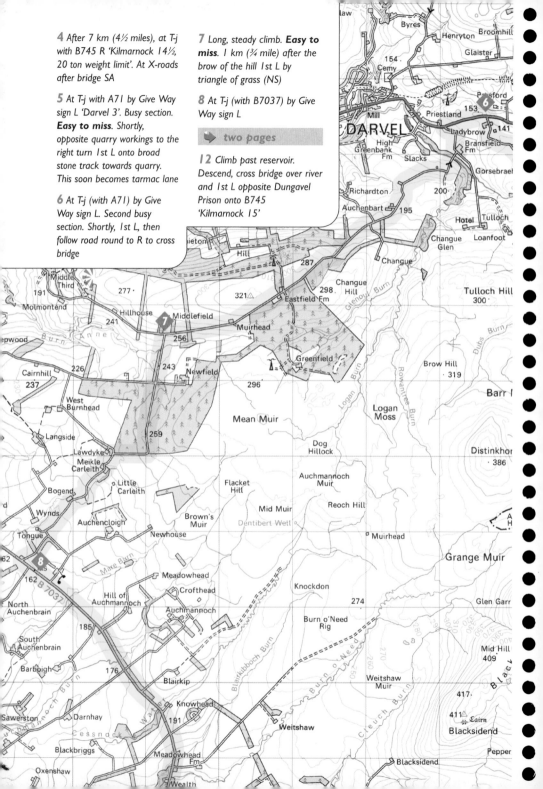

4 After 7 km (4½ miles), at T-j with B745 R 'Kilmarnock 14½, 20 ton weight limit'. At X-roads after bridge SA

5 At T-j with A71 by Give Way sign L 'Darvel 3'. Busy section. **Easy to miss**. Shortly, opposite quarry workings to the right turn 1st L onto broad stone track towards quarry. This soon becomes tarmac lane

6 At T-j (with A71) by Give Way sign L. Second busy section. Shortly, 1st L, then follow road round to R to cross bridge

7 Long, steady climb. **Easy to miss**. 1 km (¾ mile) after the brow of the hill 1st L by triangle of grass (NS)

8 At T-j (with B7037) by Give Way sign L

➡ **two pages**

12 Climb past reservoir. Descend, cross bridge over river and 1st L opposite Dungavel Prison onto B745 'Kilmarnock 15'

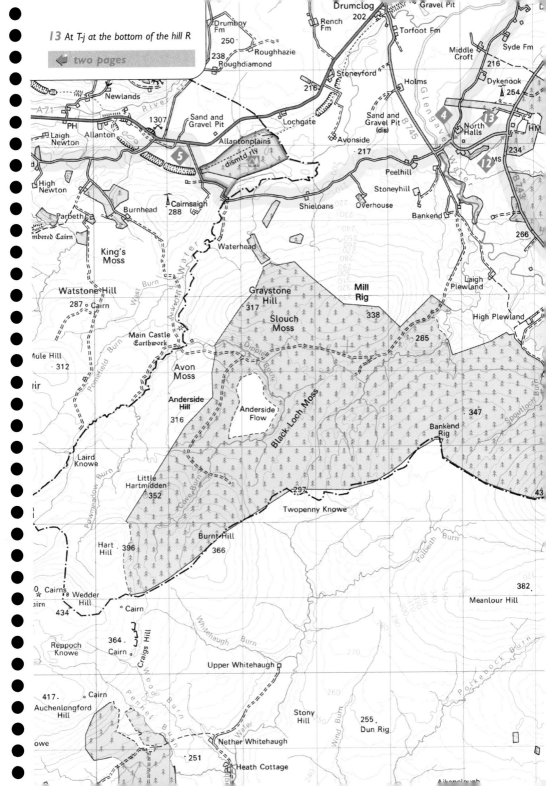

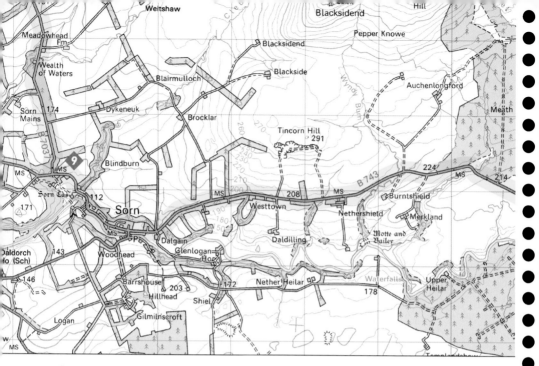

9 At T-j (with B743) L

10 Through Sorn. **Easy to miss**. Climb, descend, then climb again over 11 km (7 miles). 1 km (¾ mile) after passing Townhead of Greenock Farm on your left take the next L at X-roads 'Netherwood Farm, Burnfoot'

11 After 6½ km (4 miles) at T-j with B743 L 'Strathaven 11'

three pages

▼ Sorn Castle

Places of interest

Strathaven 1

A silk-weaving town in medieval times, some weavers' cottages still line the older streets. Powmillon Burn flows through three public parks. The gorge is dominated by a 15th-century castle ruin, below which is the Old Town Mill. This was built in 1650 by the Duke of Hamilton and functioned for 300 years, latterly used for grinding oat meal. It has now been converted into an arts centre

Sorn 9

A village laid out in 1770 on the banks of the River Ayr. The castle has a tower dating back to the 15th century. The 1650 church has an unusual outside staircase

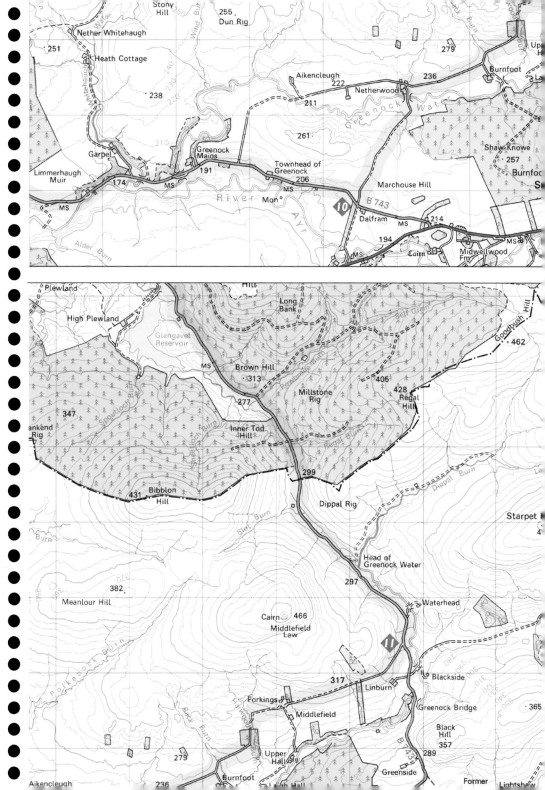

Northwest from Sanquhar through the Lowther Hills

One instinctively feels sorry for a village as dominated by a major road as Sanquhar is by the A76, taking heavy traffic from Dumfries to Kilmarnock. However, the countryside around is dramatic and beautiful, rising to over 730 m (2400 ft) on Lowther Hill, south-east of Wanlockhead, and this ride avoids the A76 almost entirely, running its course on little-used B roads. A quiet lane on the southern side of the River Nith takes you to Mennock, the start of a major climb of over 334 km (1100 ft) to Wanlockhead, the highest village in Scotland. Both Wanlockhead and Leadhills owe their existence to the mining industry, at first gold and silver, then lead. The mines have stopped working but their lives are chronicled in the museum. A long descent from the 'pass' ends when you turn off towards Crawfordjohn. However, you can enjoy a descent of some 21 km (13 miles), from the high peat moorland down through ever more wooded slopes alongside Crawick Water back to Sanquhar.

Start

Tourist Information Centre, Sanquhar

P Several small car parks

Distance and grade

51 km (32 miles)

///// Strenuous

Terrain

There is only one major climb – 350 m (1150 ft) over 12 km (7½ miles) from the River Nith near Mennock up to Leadhills. A second shorter climb of 79 m (260 ft) between the B797 after Leadhills and Crawfordjohn. Highest point – 466 m (1531 ft) at the pass between Wanlockhead and Leadhills. Lowest point – 121 m (400 ft) at the crossing of the River Nith near to Sanquhar

Nearest railway

Sanquhar

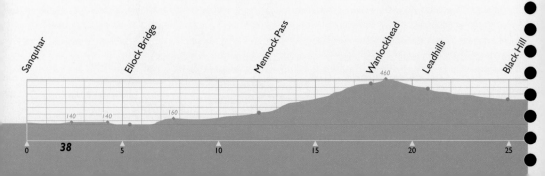

Sanquhar 1

The town Post Office, opened in 1763, survives as Britain's oldest Post Office. A granite monument pays tribute to the two declarations made by the Covenanters in 1680 and 1685, renouncing their allegiance first to Charles II, then to James VII of Scotland

Wanlockhead 5

Set 420 m (1380 feet) above sea level, it is the highest village in Scotland. Gold was once panned from neighbouring streams; indeed, gold from the area was used in the Crown of Scotland, now kept in Edinburgh Castle. The beam pump is a relic of lead-mining days. The lead mines were worked until 1934, and the disused mine is now part of the Scottish Lead Mining Museum

Leadhills 5

A hill-top graveyard has a memorial to John Taylor who died at the age of 137 after a century of working in mines. His longevity was attributed to the fresh uplands air

Below: Sanquhar, castle ruins

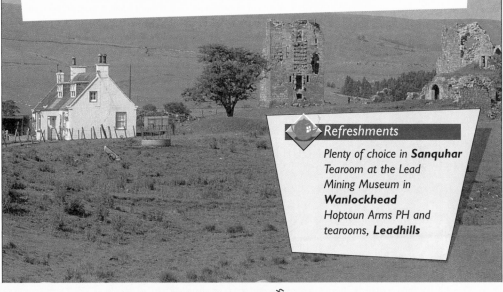

Refreshments

*Plenty of choice in **Sanquhar** Tearoom at the Lead Mining Museum in **Wanlockhead** Hoptoun Arms PH and tearooms, **Leadhills***

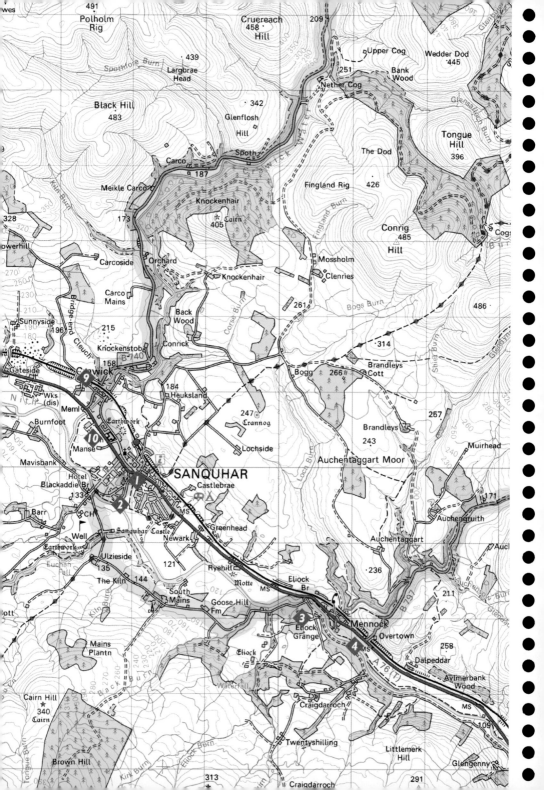

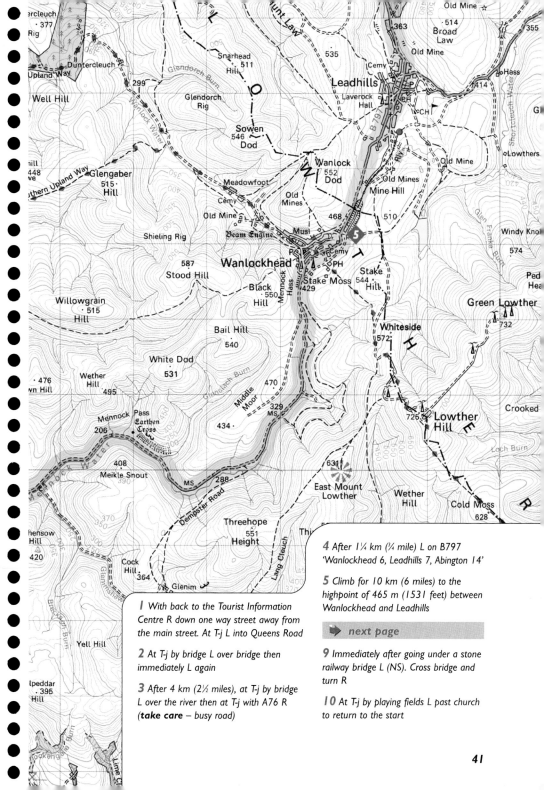

4 After 1¼ km (¾ mile) L on B797 'Wanlockhead 6, Leadhills 7, Abington 14'

5 Climb for 10 km (6 miles) to the highpoint of 465 m (1531 feet) between Wanlockhead and Leadhills

➡️ **next page**

9 Immediately after going under a stone railway bridge L (NS). Cross bridge and turn R

10 At T-j by playing fields L past church to return to the start

I With back to the Tourist Information Centre R down one way street away from the main street. At T-j L into Queens Road

2 At T-j by bridge L over bridge then immediately L again

3 After 4 km (2½ miles), at T-j by bridge L over the river then at T-j with A76 R (**take care** – busy road)

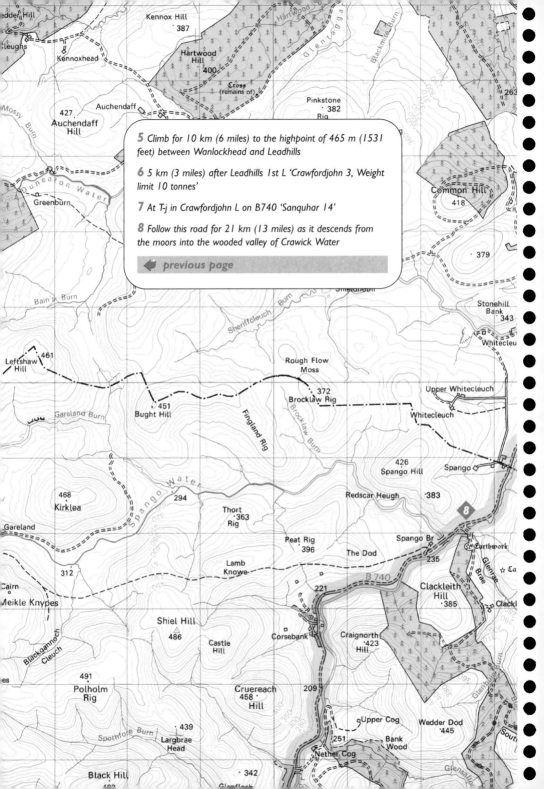

5 Climb for 10 km (6 miles) to the highpoint of 465 m (1531 feet) between Wanlockhead and Leadhills

6 5 km (3 miles) after Leadhills 1st L 'Crawfordjohn 3, Weight limit 10 tonnes'

7 At T-j in Crawfordjohn L on B740 'Sanquhar 14'

8 Follow this road for 21 km (13 miles) as it descends from the moors into the wooded valley of Crawick Water

◀ previous page

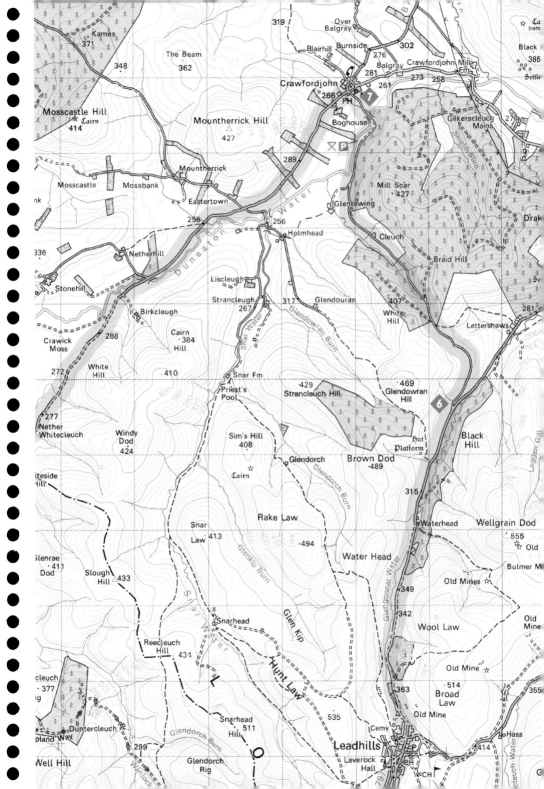

7 ⟡ Into the rolling hills west of Dumfries

No fewer than seven A roads radiate like spokes from the central hub of Dumfries, by far the largest town in Scotland south of a line from Ayr to Edinburgh. With this in mind, the same road is used to exit and re-enter Dumfries, namely, the lightly used Terregles Road. Dumfries may be a bustling commercial centre, but within 5 or 6 km (3 or 4 miles) of the town, you are in a different world of rolling farmland with stone walls and moorland broken up by forestry. It is worth diverting from the route to see the sculptures by Rodin, Epstein and Henry Moore set on the hillsides around the Glenkiln Reservoir. The road drops down through a lovely wooded section to the A712, one of the quietest A roads in the region. The route turns north, then east alongside streams called Craigenputtock Burn, Castramon Burn and Glenesslin Burn before joining Cairn Water. If there has been recent rain, the waterfalls beneath Routin Bridge will be fairly dramatic. Soon after the unusual church at Irongray, you turn south to rejoin the outward route near to Terregles.

▷ Start

Tourist Information Centre, Whitesands, Dumfries

🅿 Either along Whitesands, past the Tourist Information Centre or behind Burns House (off Brooms Road, the road towards Carlisle)

▷ Distance and grade

59 km (37 miles)
⟋⟋⟋ Moderate

▷ Terrain

Highest point – 222 m (730 ft), 6 km (4 miles) west of Shawhead. Lowest point – 6 m (20 ft) at the start, in Dumfries

▷ Nearest railway

Dumfries

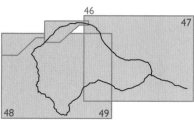

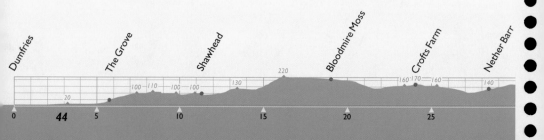

Dumfries 1

Former sea port where Robert Burns lived before his death in 1796. The Robert Burns Centre recalls his years in Dumfries and his mausoleum is in St Michael's churchyard. Mid Steeple was built in 1707 as a courthouse and prison. The 18th-century windmill contains a camera obscura and a local history museum

Glenkiln 4

Carefully placed on hillside sites northwest of Shawhead are sculptures by Epstein, Henry Moore and Rodin. They stand in the Glenkiln estate and were bought in the 1950s by the laird Sir William Keswick.

One of the most striking, and easily seen from the public road across the estate, is Epstein's 'King and Queen'. The pair gaze out over the extensive valley and moorland view near the Glenkiln Reservoir

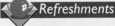 Refreshments

*Plenty of choice in **Dumfries**
Pubs just off the route in
**Kirkpatrick Durham,
Corsock** and **Dunscore***

Kirkpatrick Durham 5 *(just off the route)*

An orderly estate village little changed since it was built in 1785, with 50 houses and a number of craft workshops

Twelve Apostles Stone Circle 9 *(just off the route, east of Irongray)*

Dated 2000 BC, it is the largest diameter stone circle in Scotland. Only eleven stones remain – the twelfth was removed by locals for building

▶ Footbridge over the River Nith

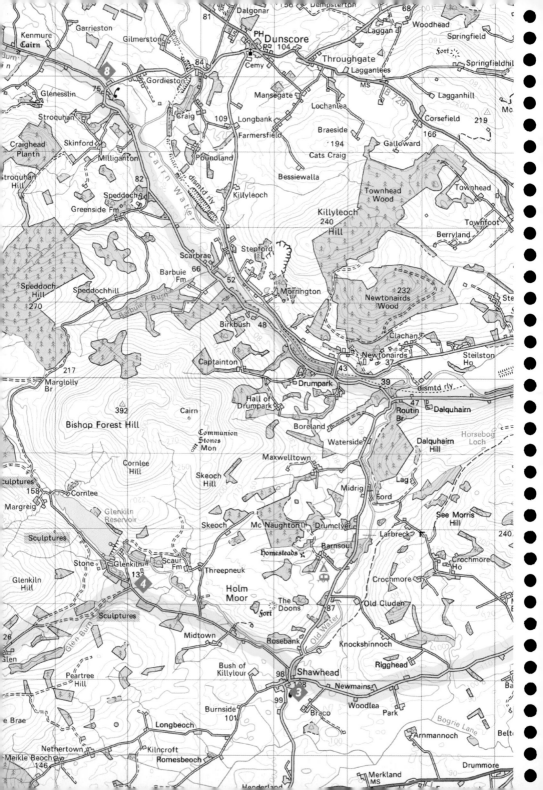

1 With back to the Tourist Information Centre L then at traffic lights L over the bridge. Ignore the A76 to the right to Kilmarnock. Take the next R on Terregles Street

2 Go past the football ground. Shortly after a petrol station and car dealership on the right, turn L by telephone box onto Terregles Road

3 Follow this road for 10 km (6 miles), ignoring left and right turns. At the start of Shawhead village turn sharply R 'Dunscore 7' then shortly 1st L by triangle of grass 'Dunscore 6' (a very short mile!)

4 After 2½ km (1½ miles), immediately after crossing a stone bridge over a stream, and 45 m (yds) before a sharp LH bend with a blue Water Board sign, turn L 'Cattle Grid' (**Or** go SA for views of the sculptures on the hillsides and return to this point)

➡️ next page

8 After 11 km (7 miles) at T-j with telephone box to the left R 'Speddoch 1, Dumfries 9'

9 Follow signs for Dumfries, ignoring a left turn to Dunscore and a right turn to Shawhead. Immediately after passing an unusual red sandstone and whitewash church on the left, turn R

10 At T-j L to rejoin outward route

11 At T-j at the end of Terregles Road by the car dealership/petrol station turn R

12 At T-j at the end of Terregles Street L. At traffic lights SA then 1st R after the bridge to return to the start

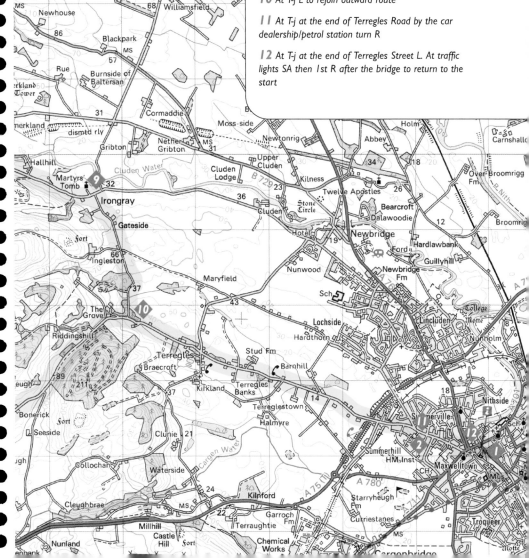

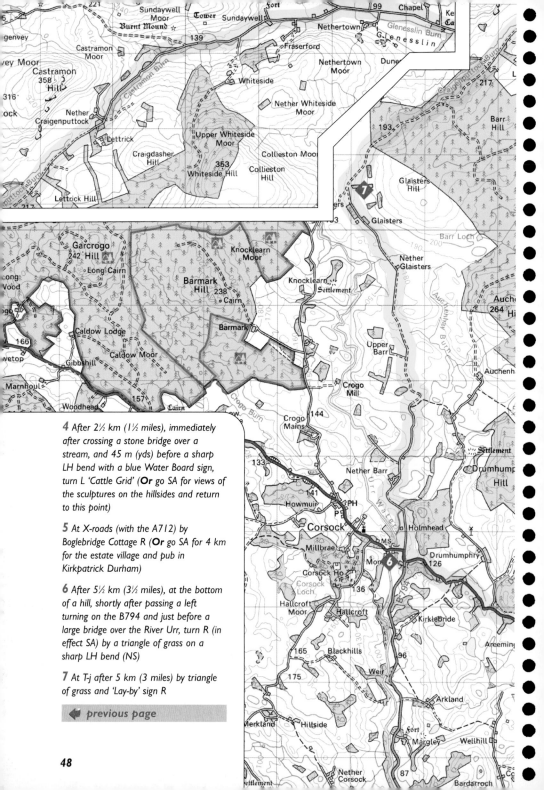

4 After 2½ km (1½ miles), immediately after crossing a stone bridge over a stream, and 45 m (yds) before a sharp LH bend with a blue Water Board sign, turn L 'Cattle Grid' (**Or** go SA for views of the sculptures on the hillsides and return to this point)

5 At X-roads (with the A712) by Boglebridge Cottage R (**Or** go SA for 4 km for the estate village and pub in Kirkpatrick Durham)

6 After 5½ km (3½ miles), at the bottom of a hill, shortly after passing a left turning on the B794 and just before a large bridge over the River Urr, turn R (in effect SA) by a triangle of grass on a sharp LH bend (NS)

7 At T-j after 5 km (3 miles) by triangle of grass and 'Lay-by' sign R

◀ previous page

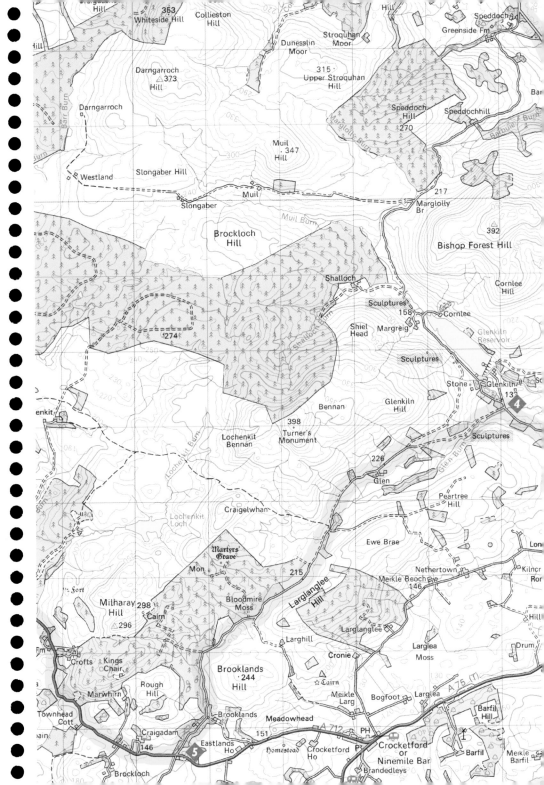

⬧8⬧ From Kirkcudbright to Castle Douglas via Palnackie

Start

The bridge over the River Dee, Kirkcudbright

P Some parking in the square by the Tourist Information Centre

Distance and grade

56 km (35 miles)

Moderate

Terrain

121 m (400 ft) climb from the start to Dundrennan, steep 91 m (300 ft) climb north from Palnackie, and a 85 m (280 ft) climb from Castle

Most of the A roads in the southwest of Scotland, with the exception of the A75, A76 and A77, carry very little traffic and are appropriate for leisure cycling. This is particularly useful to know in the case of the roads that run parallel with the coast, as they boast some magnificent views, in this case across the Solway Firth towards the fells of the Lake District. The ride starts by following Kirkcudbright Bay south through Mutehill with views across to the light-house on the island of Little

Ross. Once the A711 is rejoined, there are several reasons for stopping or detouring: the ruins of the abbey at Dundrennan, a side trip out along Auchencairn Bay to the Balcary Bay Hotel or the Tower at Orchardton Mains shortly before Palnackie. If visibility is good, you should enjoy excellent views of the Lake District, particularly between Auchencairn and Palnackie. From here the route cuts north, climbing steeply for a short while before dropping down to Castle Douglas that offers a wide choice of refreshments and some culture in the form of the National Trust property of Threave Gardens. A steady climb from Threave is followed by an 8 km (5 mile) descent back into Kirkcudbright.

Kirkcudbright | The Lake | Drummore Castle | Townhead | Dundrennan | Bankhead | Auchencairn

50 — 70—80 — 90— 120 — 120 — 40 — 20

Douglas to the ride's highest point halfway back to Kirkcudbright. Highest point – 131 m (430 ft) on the B727 between Castle Douglas and Kirkcudbright. Lowest point – sea level at the start

Nearest railway

Dumfries, 29 km (18 miles) east of Castle Douglas

Places of interest

Dundrennan Abbey 4
A handsome and substantial Cistercian ruin, founded in 1142, where Mary, Queen of Scots, spent her last night in Scotland in 1568

Auchencairn Bay 5
Pebble beaches become acres of sand at low tide. Smugglers built Balcary House in Auchencairn Bay in the 18th century to store contraband. Beyond the bay is one of the finest footpaths of the Solway Coast, leading to spectacular cliffs where rock stacks plunge dizzily down to the sea

Orchardton Tower 5
A round tower house, unique in Scotland, built in the 15th century by John Cairns. It contains a spiral staircase hidden within double walls, leading to a parapet walk

Palnackie 6
A village little changed since its days as a thriving inland port. The harbour is now silted up. Granite from the nearby Craignair quarries was shipped from here and used in the building of Liverpool Docks, the Thames Embankment and Manchester Town Hall. Competitors use bare feet and spears to catch fish from the mud flats off Glen Isle peninsula in the World Flounder Tramping Championship

Castle Douglas 9
In the 18th century, the town was a weaving and carpet-making centre

Threave Gardens and Wildlife Refuge 11
The estate surrounding the Scottish baronial Threave House has woodland walks and various gardens. On an island to the northwest is ruined Threave Castle, the 14th-century stronghold of the feared Black Douglases

Refreshments

Plenty of choice in **Kirkcudbright**
Crown and Anchor PH, **Dundrennan**
Solwayside House Hotel, Old Smugglers Inn ●,
Auchencairn
Balcary Bay Hotel, ●● (off the route, southeast of **Auchencairn,** worth the diversion)
Glenisle Inn, **Palnackie**

Gardenburn · Castle Douglas · Rhonehouse or Kelton Hill · Little Sypland

20 · 90 · 90 · 110 · 60 · 60 · 60 · 70 · 90 · 100 · 130 · 130 · 10

30 · 35 · 40 · 45 · 50 · **51** · 55 · 56

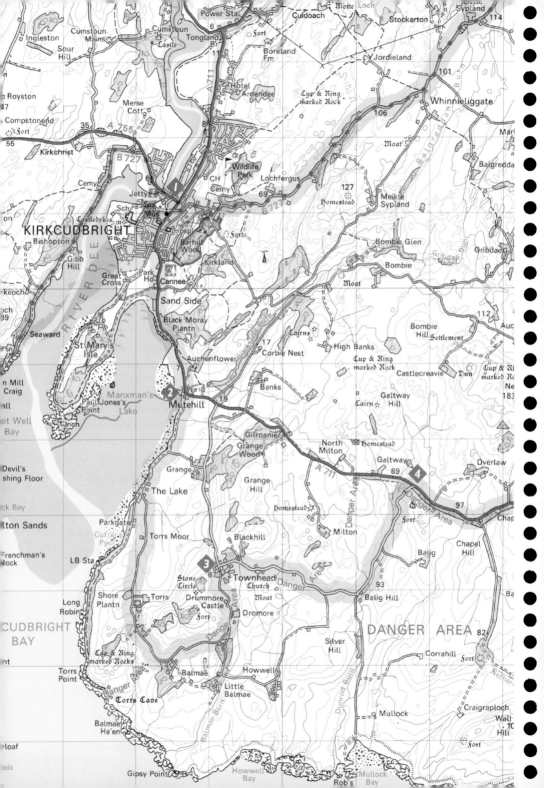

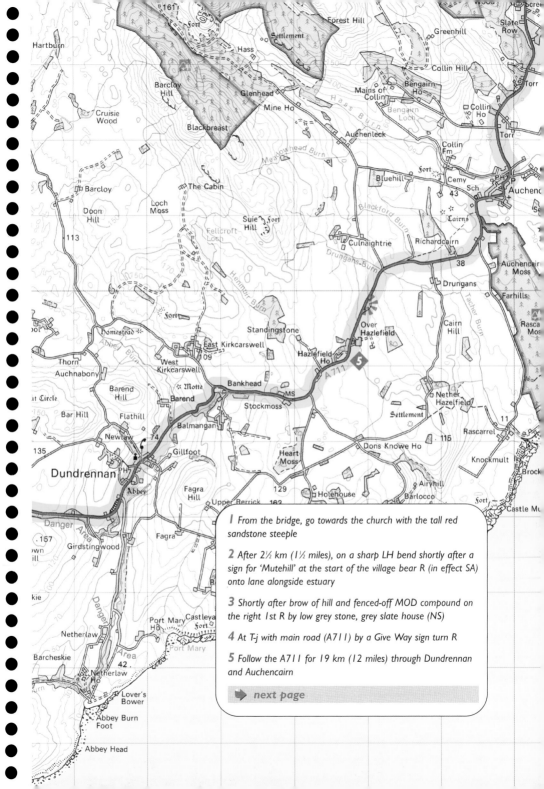

1 From the bridge, go towards the church with the tall red sandstone steeple

2 After 2½ km (1½ miles), on a sharp LH bend shortly after a sign for 'Mutehill' at the start of the village bear R (in effect SA) onto lane alongside estuary

3 Shortly after brow of hill and fenced-off MOD compound on the right 1st R by low grey stone, grey slate house (NS)

4 At T-j with main road (A711) by a Give Way sign turn R

5 Follow the A711 for 19 km (12 miles) through Dundrennan and Auchencairn

➡ next page

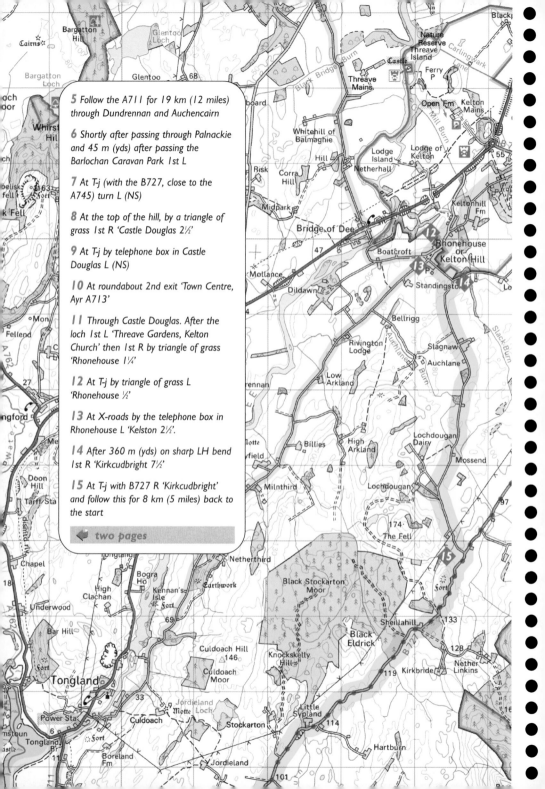

5 Follow the A711 for 19 km (12 miles) through Dundrennan and Auchencairn

6 Shortly after passing through Palnackie and 45 m (yds) after passing the Barlochan Caravan Park 1st L

7 At T-j (with the B727, close to the A745) turn L (NS)

8 At the top of the hill, by a triangle of grass 1st R 'Castle Douglas 2½'

9 At T-j by telephone box in Castle Douglas L (NS)

10 At roundabout 2nd exit 'Town Centre, Ayr A713'

11 Through Castle Douglas. After the loch 1st L 'Threave Gardens, Kelton Church' then 1st R by triangle of grass 'Rhonehouse 1¼'

12 At T-j by triangle of grass L 'Rhonehouse ½'

13 At X-roads by the telephone box in Rhonehouse L 'Kelston 2½'.

14 After 360 m (yds) on sharp LH bend 1st R 'Kirkcudbright 7½'

15 At T-j with B727 R 'Kirkcudbright' and follow this for 8 km (5 miles) back to the start

two pages

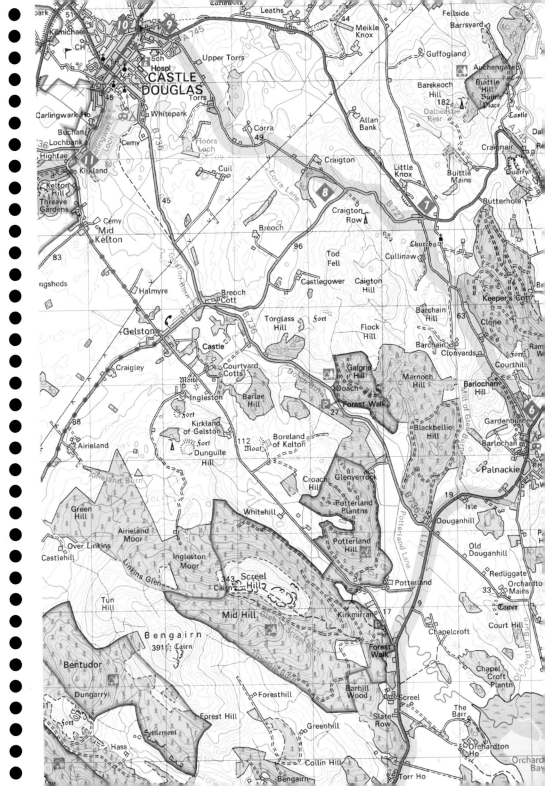

Kirkcudbright to Gatehouse of Fleet via Laurieston Forest

Leaving the attractions of Kirkcudbright, the ride follows the River Dee north through lanes of high hedgerows and wildflowers reminiscent of Shropshire or Devon. The Dee and the busy A75 are crossed at Bridge of Dee and you soon pass the ruins of Threave Castle on your right, once home of the infamous Black Douglases. West from Laurieston, the route climbs through Laurieston Forest, which has been thoughtfully managed to give the illusion of riding through broadleaf woodland for much of the time. Views start opening up of the Cairnsmore of Fleet away to the west, rising to over 608 m (2000 ft). Once out of the forest, the views become even more impressive: Wigtown Bay is spread out before you. A long, exhilarating descent drops you in Gatehouse of Fleet before heading south to Borgue and then following the shore of Kirkcudbright Bay back to the start.

Start

The bridge over the River Dee in Kirkcudbright

P Some parking in the square by the Tourist Information Centre

Distance and grade

59 km (37 miles)

Moderate

Terrain

70 m (230 ft) climb between Kirkcudbright and Bridge of Dee. 167 m (550 ft) from

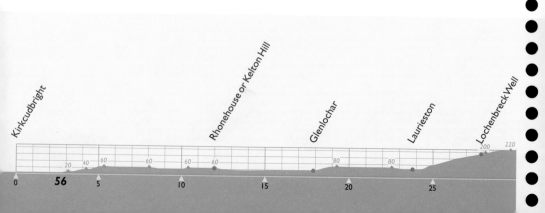

Kirkcudbright · Rhonehouse or Kelton Hill · Glenlochar · Laurieston · Lochenbreck Well

20 40 60 60 60 60 80 80 200 220

0   56   5   10   15   20   25

Glenlochar west to the highpoint in Laurieston Forest. 76 m (250 ft) climb between Gatehouse of Fleet and Borgue. Highest point – 213 m (700 ft) in the heart of Laurieston Forest. Lowest point – sea level in Kirkcudbright and Gatehouse of Fleet

Nearest railway

Dumfries, 32 km (20 miles) east of the route at Bridge of Dee

Places of interest

Kirkcudbright 1
The town is dominated by St Cuthbert's church spire, the Gothic tower of Tolbooth and the jagged top of the 16th-century MacLellann's Castle. The wooded Wildlife Park has eagle, snowy and barn owls. Broughton House, an elegant Georgian mansion with gardens on the River Dee, houses a museum and art gallery

Tongland 2
Battlemented and turreted bridge over River Dee, designed by Thomas Telford in the 1800s. There are guided tours around the hydroelectric power station and dam, which has 29 pools in its salmon ladder

Gatehouse of Fleet 9
The original gatehouse now houses a whitewashed wine bar. The Bobbin Mill Visitor Centre displays local history and recalls its 18th-century prosperity as a cotton town

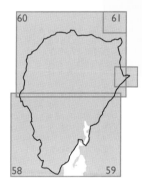

Refreshments

*Plenty of choice in **Kirkcudbright** Laurie Arms PH, **Laurieston** Murray Arms PH ●●, lots of choice in **Gatehouse of Fleet***

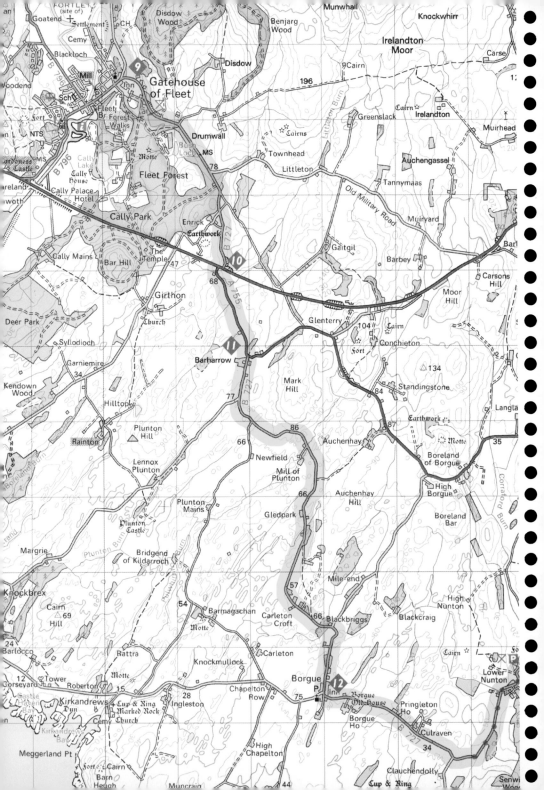

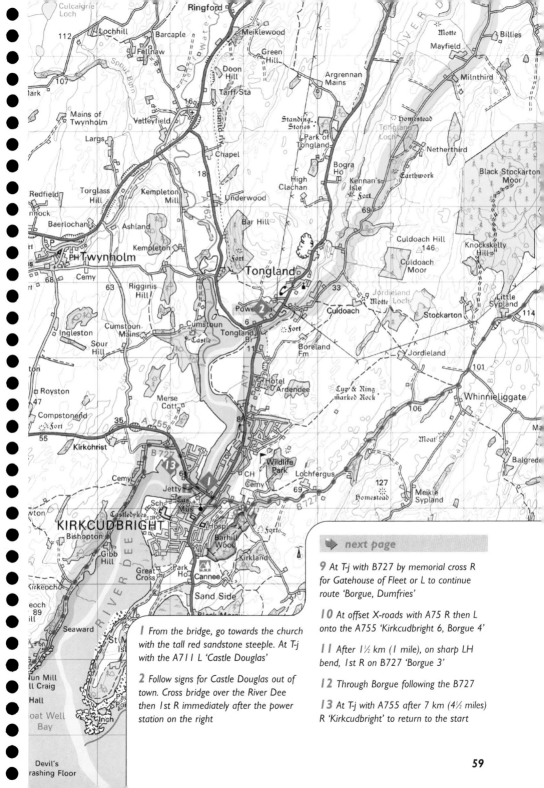

➡ **next page**

9 At T-j with B727 by memorial cross R for Gatehouse of Fleet or L to continue route 'Borgue, Dumfries'

10 At offset X-roads with A75 R then L onto the A755 'Kirkcudbright 6, Borgue 4'

11 After 1½ km (1 mile), on sharp LH bend, 1st R on B727 'Borgue 3'

12 Through Borgue following the B727

13 At T-j with A755 after 7 km (4½ miles) R 'Kirkcudbright' to return to the start

1 From the bridge, go towards the church with the tall red sandstone steeple. At T-j with the A711 L 'Castle Douglas'

2 Follow signs for Castle Douglas out of town. Cross bridge over the River Dee then 1st R immediately after the power station on the right

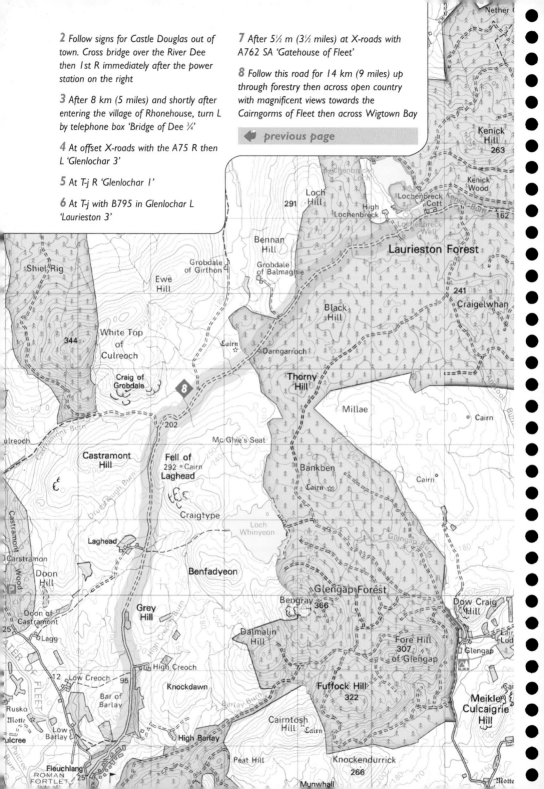

2 Follow signs for Castle Douglas out of town. Cross bridge over the River Dee then 1st R immediately after the power station on the right

3 After 8 km (5 miles) and shortly after entering the village of Rhonehouse, turn L by telephone box 'Bridge of Dee ¾'

4 At offset X-roads with the A75 R then L 'Glenlochar 3'

5 At T-j R 'Glenlochar 1'

6 At T-j with B795 in Glenlochar L 'Laurieston 3'

7 After 5½ m (3½ miles) at X-roads with A762 SA 'Gatehouse of Fleet'

8 Follow this road for 14 km (9 miles) up through forestry then across open country with magnificent views towards the Cairngorms of Fleet then across Wigtown Bay

◀ *previous page*

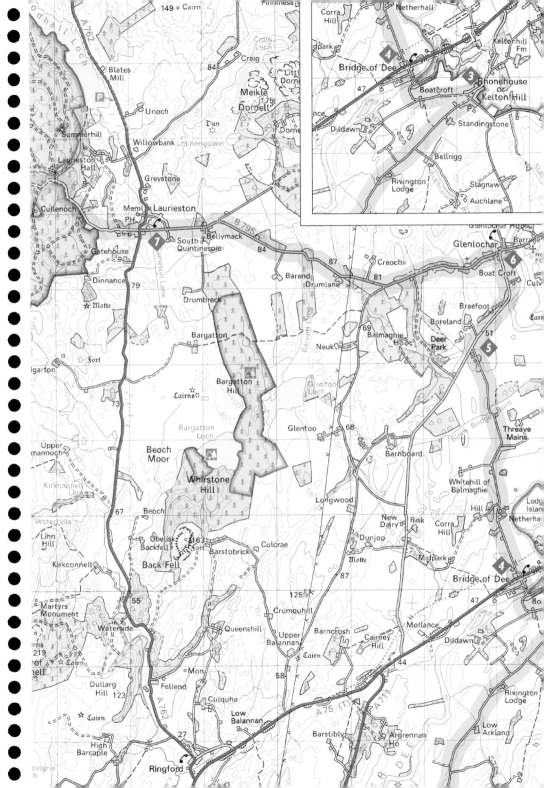

South from Wigtown to early Christian settlements at Whithorn

This is a very easy ride, with no major climbs and some wonderful sea views together with a visit to Whithorn, an important archaeological site for early Christian and Viking discoveries. The ride stays as close to the shore of Wigtown Bay as possible on the outward route, touching the sea at the small harbour of Garlieston. There are fine views out to sea from the Isle of Whithorn, and McWilliams stores would do well in the Leaning Tower of Pisa stakes. Whithorn is the central community for the whole peninsula and has displays of what has been found to date in the Whithorn Dig. Quiet lanes are followed north to Whauphill where the A714 is joined on the return to Wigtown.

Start

The County Hotel, Wigtown, 40 km (25 miles) east of Stranraer

P In the main square

Distance and grade

56 km (35 miles)
Easy

Terrain

Gentle 79 m (260 ft) climb over 8 km (5 miles) northwest from the Isle of Whithorn. Highest point – 79 m (260 ft), west of Whithorn. Lowest point – sea level, Bladnoch, Garlieston and Isle of Whithorn

Nearest railway

Stranraer, 40 km (25 miles) west of Wigtown

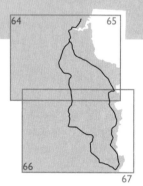

Refreshments

Plenty of choice in **Wigtown**
Bladnoch Inn, **Bladnoch**
Queens Arms PH, Harbour Inn ✦,
coffee shop, **Garlieston**
Steam Packet Inn ✦✦,
Queens Arms Hotel, **Isle of Whithorn**
Plenty of choice in **Whithorn**
Whauphill Hotel, **Whauphill**

Wigtown · Braehead · Kirkinner · Garlieston · Portyerrock · Isle of Whithorn

40 20 50 30 20 30 30 20

0   5   10   15   20   25

Wigtown 1

The Martyrs' Memorial Stone marks the spot where two Presbyterian women who refused to recant their religion were, in 1685, tied to stakes in the River Bladnoch to drown in the rising tide

Garlieston 4

For a long time the village was in the curious position of being a port without a harbour: rivers flowing into the sea here silted up the coast, so boats had to anchor in the nearest stretch of deep water, and smaller boats were then used to take passengers and cargo ashore. Eventually, in the 19th century, a proper harbour was built and ships called in on runs from London, Liverpool and Dublin

Galloway House Gardens 4 (south of Garlieston)

Laid out in the 1740s as pleasure gardens for Galloway House, they include the rare handkerchief tree and a heronry

Isle of Whithorn 8

A busy sailing resort where St Ninian landed on the grassy peninsula in AD 395 on his return from Rome. There is also an Iron Age fort and a ruined 13th-century chapel

Whithorn 10

The 12th-century priory ruin, said to be built on the site of St Ninian's 5th-century church Candida Casa, or 'white house', retains a barrel-vaulted crypt and a roofless nave. The site has been excavated to reveal the foundations of a Viking Trading settlement, coins and gaming pieces from earlier times

▲ Wigtown 'Harbour', River Bladnoch

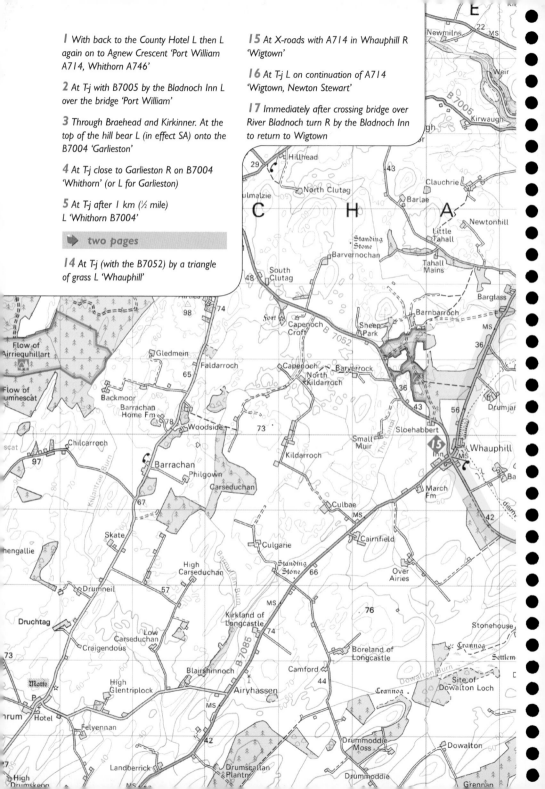

1 With back to the County Hotel L then L again on to Agnew Crescent 'Port William A714, Whithorn A746'

2 At T-j with B7005 by the Bladnoch Inn L over the bridge 'Port William'

3 Through Braehead and Kirkinner. At the top of the hill bear L (in effect SA) onto the B7004 'Garlieston'

4 At T-j close to Garlieston R on B7004 'Whithorn' (or L for Garlieston)

5 At T-j after I km (½ mile) L 'Whithorn B7004'

➡ two pages

14 At T-j (with the B7052) by a triangle of grass L 'Whauphill'

15 At X-roads with A714 in Whauphill R 'Wigtown'

16 At T-j L on continuation of A714 'Wigtown, Newton Stewart'

17 Immediately after crossing bridge over River Bladnoch turn R by the Bladnoch Inn to return to Wigtown

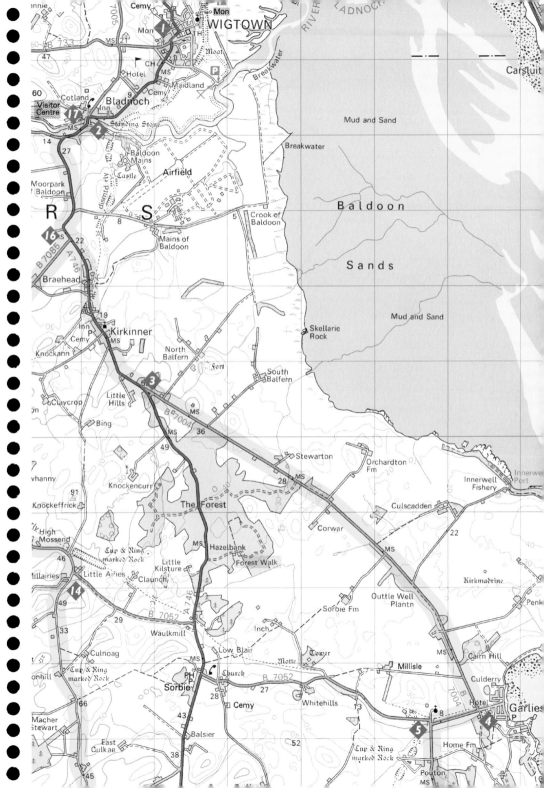

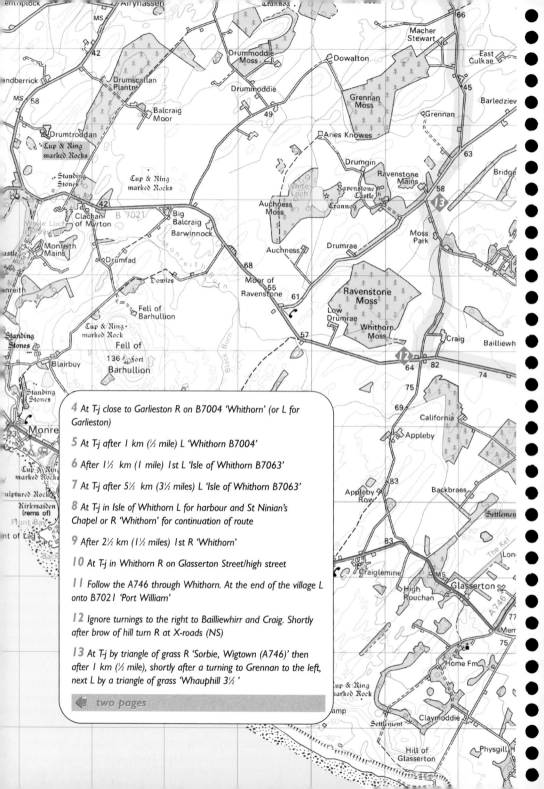

4 At T-j close to Garlieston R on B7004 'Whithorn' (or L for Garlieston)

5 At T-j after 1 km (½ mile) L 'Whithorn B7004'

6 After 1½ km (1 mile) 1st L 'Isle of Whithorn B7063'

7 At T-j after 5½ km (3½ miles) L 'Isle of Whithorn B7063'

8 At T-j in Isle of Whithorn L for harbour and St Ninian's Chapel or R 'Whithorn' for continuation of route

9 After 2½ km (1½ miles) 1st R 'Whithorn'

10 At T-j in Whithorn R on Glasserton Street/high street

11 Follow the A746 through Whithorn. At the end of the village L onto B7021 'Port William'

12 Ignore turnings to the right to Bailliewhirr and Craig. Shortly after brow of hill turn R at X-roads (NS)

13 At T-j by triangle of grass R 'Sorbie, Wigtown (A746)' then after 1 km (½ mile), shortly after a turning to Grennan to the left, next L by a triangle of grass 'Whauphill 3½'

◄ *two pages*

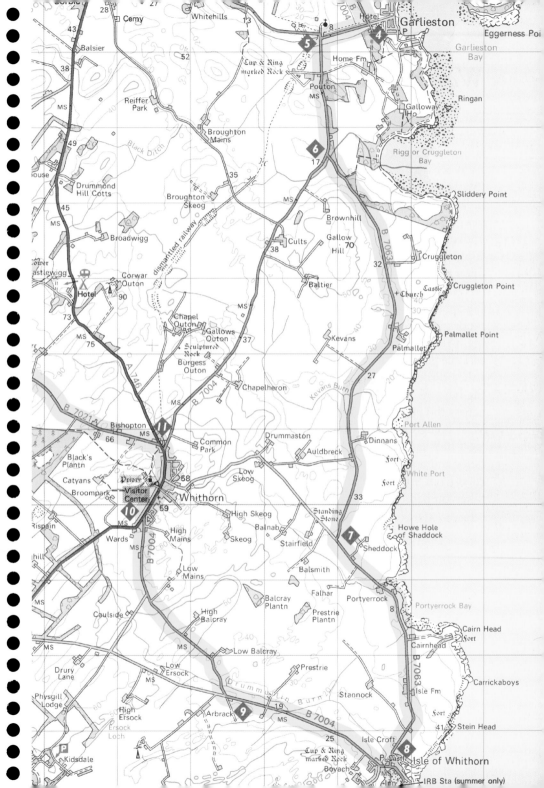

Stranraer and the Water of Luce

Stranraer is dominated by the Northern Ireland ferry terminal. However, its setting is beautiful, with hills rising to 213 m (700 ft) as a backdrop to Loch Ryan. The route follows the side of the loch for 4 km (2½ miles) before climbing Braid Fell over the next 4 km (2½ miles) onto the moorland above the town. If you need any excuse to stop, simply turn around and see the views opening up across Loch Ryan to the Rhins, the piece of land to the west of Stranraer. Big views and skies above the heather moorland give way, as you start descending, to a more wooded aspect as the Water of Luce gathers volume and cuts a sharper valley through the hills. In order to avoid the busy A75, the route heads southwest across the pine-planted flatlands near to West Freugh airfield with its distinctive 'golf ball' communications building. Quiet lanes and a section along the old military road from Stranraer to Newton Stewart take you back into Stranraer.

Start

Salvation Army Centre by the roundabout and petrol station near the ferry port, Stranraer

P Long-stay car park on the A718 towards Kirkholm

Distance and grade

51 km (32 miles)
Moderate

Terrain

There is only one major climb, of 213 m (700 ft) over 4 km (2½ miles), near to the start. The rest is downhill or relatively flat. Highest point – 213 m (700 ft) on Braid Fell northeast of Stranraer. Lowest point – sea level, at the start

Nearest railway

Stranraer

Stranraer 1

Ferry terminal for Larne, Northern Ireland. The Castle of St John is now a visitor centre. North West Castle, shaped like a ship, was home of the 18th-century polar explorer Sir John Ross

Castle Kennedy Gardens 12 *(just off the route)*

The gardens, encompassing two castles, were laid out by Field Marshal Lord Stair and his troops in the 18th century. They feature terraces, a lily pond and separate gardens of the Stair family's castle Lochinch

Glenluce 5

(just off the route)
The 16th-century Castle of Park to the west over-looks the village from across the Water of Luce. The 12th-century Cistercian abbey ruins retain a chapter house with vaulted ceiling and Gothic windows

Soulseat Loch 11/12

Near the loch is the promontory site of a herb garden, planted besides the remains of Soulseat Abbey, featuring 100 species set in individual beds

▲ *Stranraer*

Refreshments

Plenty of choice in **Stranraer**
Kenmuir Arms Hotel,
New Luce

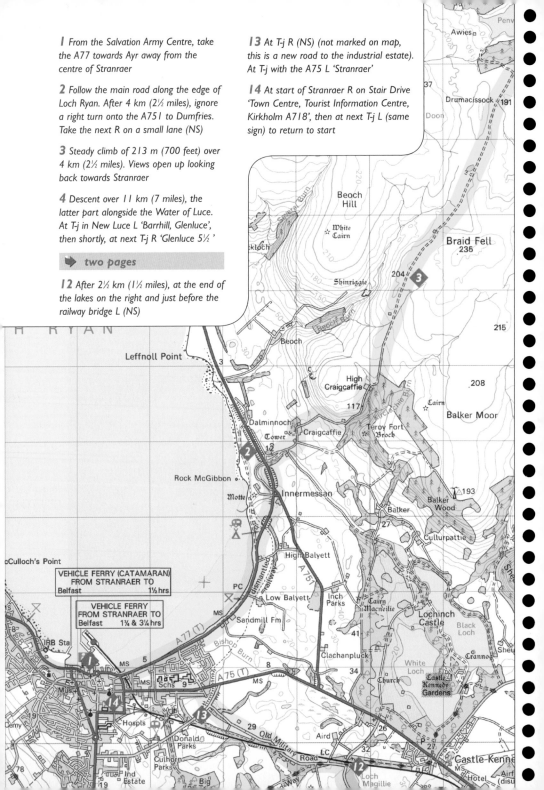

1 From the Salvation Army Centre, take the A77 towards Ayr away from the centre of Stranraer

2 Follow the main road along the edge of Loch Ryan. After 4 km (2½ miles), ignore a right turn onto the A751 to Dumfries. Take the next R on a small lane (NS)

3 Steady climb of 213 m (700 feet) over 4 km (2½ miles). Views open up looking back towards Stranraer

4 Descent over 11 km (7 miles), the latter part alongside the Water of Luce. At T-j in New Luce L 'Barrhill, Glenluce', then shortly, at next T-j R 'Glenluce 5½'

➡ **two pages**

12 After 2½ km (1½ miles), at the end of the lakes on the right and just before the railway bridge L (NS)

13 At T-j R (NS) (not marked on map, this is a new road to the industrial estate). At T-j with the A75 L 'Stranraer'

14 At start of Stranraer R on Stair Drive 'Town Centre, Tourist Information Centre, Kirkholm A718', then at next T-j L (same sign) to return to start

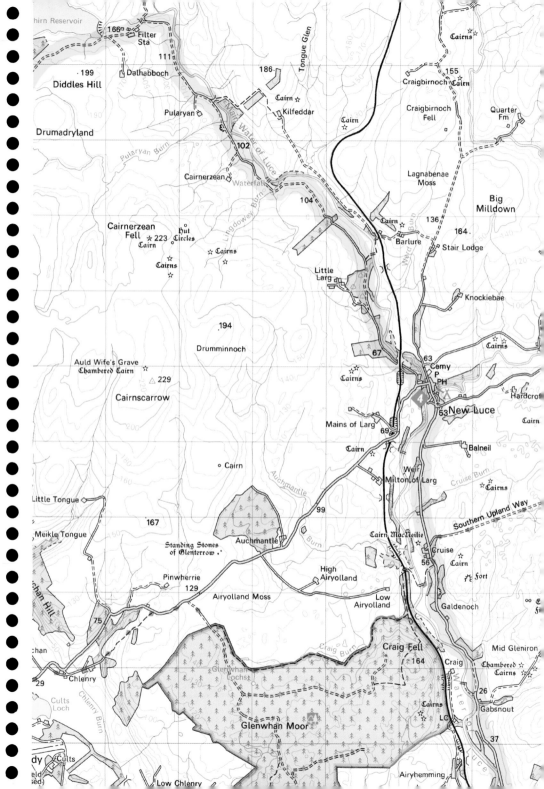

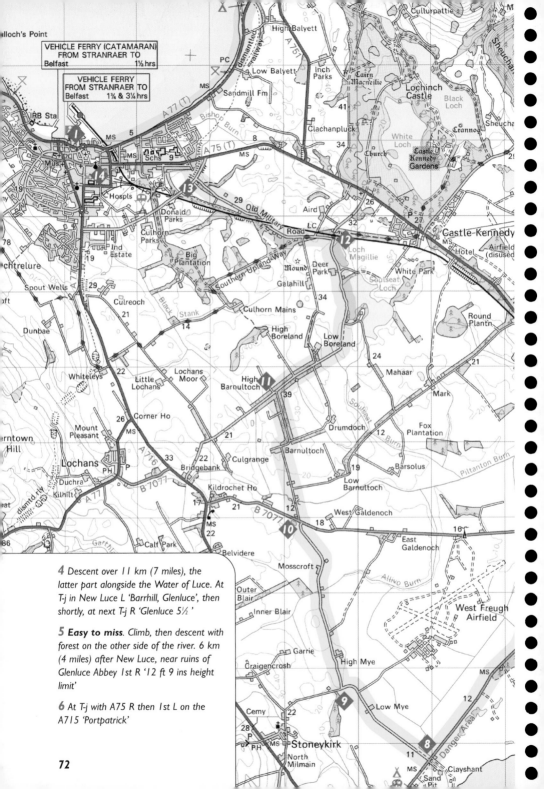

VEHICLE FERRY (CATAMARAN) FROM STRANRAER TO
Belfast   1½ hrs

VEHICLE FERRY FROM STRANRAER TO
Belfast   1¼ & 3¼ hrs

4 *Descent over 11 km (7 miles), the latter part alongside the Water of Luce. At T-j in New Luce L 'Barrhill, Glenluce', then shortly, at next T-j R 'Glenluce 5½ '*

5 **Easy to miss**. *Climb, then descent with forest on the other side of the river. 6 km (4 miles) after New Luce, near ruins of Glenluce Abbey 1st R '12 ft 9 ins height limit'*

6 *At T-j with A75 R then 1st L on the A715 'Portpatrick'*

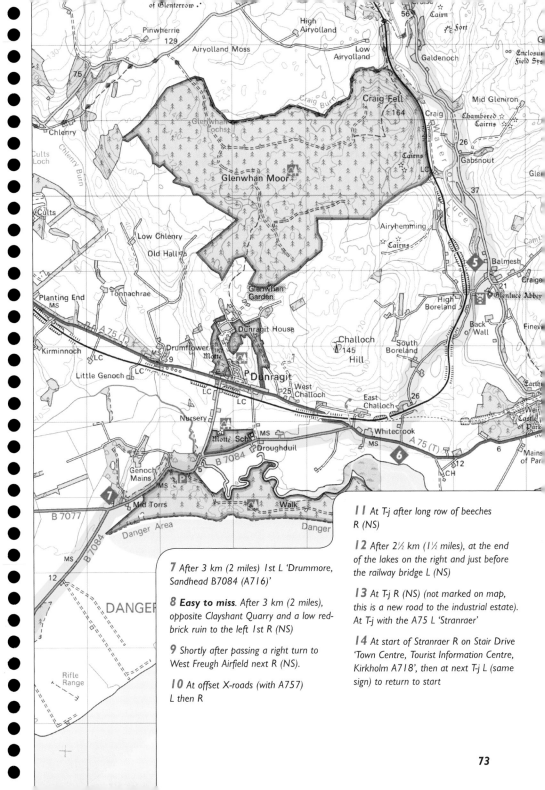

7 After 3 km (2 miles) 1st L 'Drummore, Sandhead B7084 (A716)'

8 Easy to miss. After 3 km (2 miles), opposite Clayshant Quarry and a low red-brick ruin to the left 1st R (NS)

9 Shortly after passing a right turn to West Freugh Airfield next R (NS).

10 At offset X-roads (with A757) L then R

11 At T-j after long row of beeches R (NS)

12 After 2½ km (1½ miles), at the end of the lakes on the right and just before the railway bridge L (NS)

13 At T-j R (NS) (not marked on map, this is a new road to the industrial estate). At T-j with the A75 L 'Stranraer'

14 At start of Stranraer R on Stair Drive 'Town Centre, Tourist Information Centre, Kirkholm A718', then at next T-j L (same sign) to return to start

West from Stranraer across The Rhins to Portpatrick

Start

Salvation Army Centre by the roundabout on the seafront, Stranraer

P Long-stay car park on the A718

Distance and grade

51 km (32 miles)

Easy/moderate

Terrain

91 m (300 ft) climb from Sandhead towards Portpatrick and a 103 m (340 foot) climb north of Portpatrick. Highest point – 121 m (400 ft) on the narrow coastal road between Sandhead and Portpatrick. Lowest point – sea level at Stranraer and Portpatrick

Nearest railway

Stranraer

*T*he peninsula of The Rhins lying to the west of Stranraer provides many cycling opportunities, most obviously a ride from one end to the other, from the lighthouse at the Mull of Galloway in the south to the lighthouse at Corsewall Point in the north, a one-way trip of some 56 km (35 miles). The ride leaves Stranraer to the south and passes through a line of lovely smooth-limbed beech trees near to the farm at High Barnultoch. West of Sandhead you follow the delightful lane through Cairngarroch and Kirklauchline with ever better views of the sea to the west. The caravan sites near to Portpatrick strike a slightly incongruous note but Portpatrick itself is a jewel of a village with a very good pub as an extra enticement. North from Portpatrick the route aims for Leswalt, passing through a veritable forest of rhododendron trees around Lochnaw Castle. After Leswalt, there are fine views over Loch Ryan on the return to Stranraer.

76
77
78
79

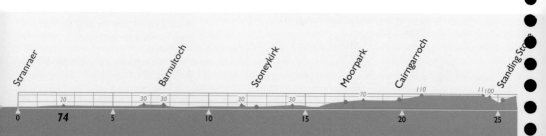

Stranraer
Barnultoch
Stoneykirk
Moorpark
Cairngarroch
Standing Sto

20
30
30
30
30
70
110
11100

0
74
5
10
15
20
25

▲ *Old church tower, Portpatrick*

Places of interest

Portpatrick 13

The town used to be the terminus of the main ferry route between Scotland and Northern Ireland, and its harbour was extended in 1821. However, the harbour was severely damaged by south-westerly gales and the steamer service was transferred to Stranraer. The 17th-century parish church, now in ruins, was used for eloping couples. Many of them came from Northern Ireland, just 35 km (22 miles) away across the sea

Portpatrick
Knock & Maize
HalfMark
Leswalt

120   60   100   100   80   80   80   90   120
10
30   35   40   45   75   52

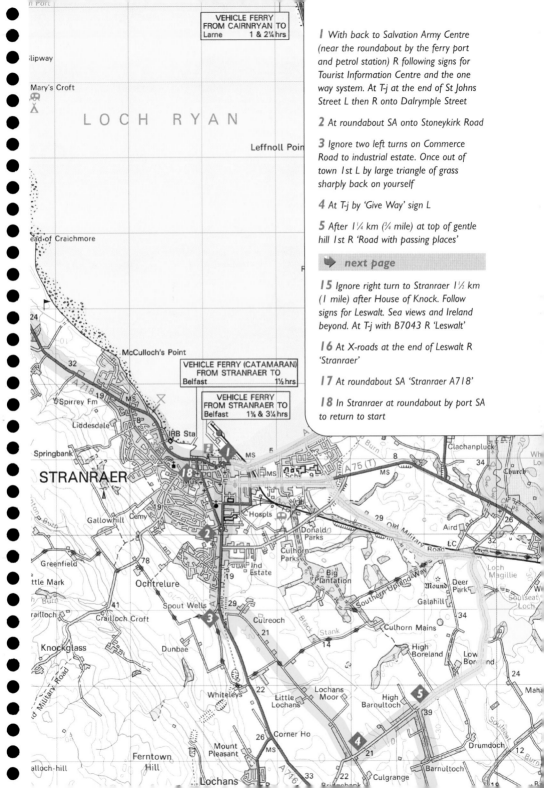

VEHICLE FERRY FROM CAIRNRYAN TO
Larne   1 & 2¼ hrs

1 With back to Salvation Army Centre (near the roundabout by the ferry port and petrol station) R following signs for Tourist Information Centre and the one way system. At T-j at the end of St Johns Street L then R onto Dalrymple Street

2 At roundabout SA onto Stoneykirk Road

3 Ignore two left turns on Commerce Road to industrial estate. Once out of town 1st L by large triangle of grass sharply back on yourself

4 At T-j by 'Give Way' sign L

5 After 1¼ km (¾ mile) at top of gentle hill 1st R 'Road with passing places'

➡ **next page**

15 Ignore right turn to Stranraer 1½ km (1 mile) after House of Knock. Follow signs for Leswalt. Sea views and Ireland beyond. At T-j with B7043 R 'Leswalt'

16 At X-roads at the end of Leswalt R 'Stranraer'

17 At roundabout SA 'Stranraer A718'

18 In Stranraer at roundabout by port SA to return to start

VEHICLE FERRY (CATAMARAN) FROM STRANRAER TO
Belfast   1½ hrs

VEHICLE FERRY FROM STRANRAER TO
Belfast   1¾ & 3¼ hrs

LOCH RYAN

Mary's Croft

Leffnoll Point

ead of Craichmore

McCulloch's Point

Spirrey Fm

Liddesdale

IRB Sta

Springbank

STRANRAER

Gallowhill   Cemy

Greenfield

ttle Mark   Ochtrelure

railloch   Crailloch Croft   Spout Wells

Knockglass   Dunbae

Whiteleys

Mount Pleasant

Ferntown Hill

alloch-hill   Lochans

Donald Parks

Ind Estate

Culhorn Parks

Hospls

Big Plantation

Culreoch

Stank

Little Lochans

Lochans Moor

Corner Ho

Culgrange

Clachanpluck

Church

Aird

Old Military Road

Southern Upland Way

Mound   Deer Park

Galahill

Culhorn Mains

High Boreland   Low Boreland

High Barnultoch

Drumdoch

Barnultoch

Loch Magillie

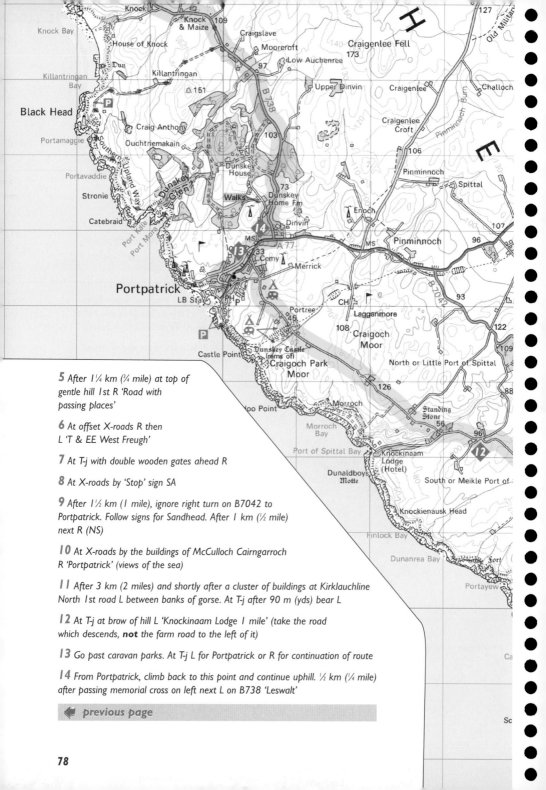

5 After 1¼ km (¾ mile) at top of gentle hill 1st R 'Road with passing places'

6 At offset X-roads R then L 'T & EE West Freugh'

7 At T-j with double wooden gates ahead R

8 At X-roads by 'Stop' sign SA

9 After 1½ km (1 mile), ignore right turn on B7042 to Portpatrick. Follow signs for Sandhead. After 1 km (½ mile) next R (NS)

10 At X-roads by the buildings of McCulloch Cairngarroch R 'Portpatrick' (views of the sea)

11 After 3 km (2 miles) and shortly after a cluster of buildings at Kirklauchline North 1st road L between banks of gorse. At T-j after 90 m (yds) bear L

12 At T-j at brow of hill L 'Knockinaam Lodge 1 mile' (take the road which descends, **not** the farm road to the left of it)

13 Go past caravan parks. At T-j L for Portpatrick or R for continuation of route

14 From Portpatrick, climb back to this point and continue uphill. ½ km (¼ mile) after passing memorial cross on left next L on B738 'Leswalt'

◀ *previous page*

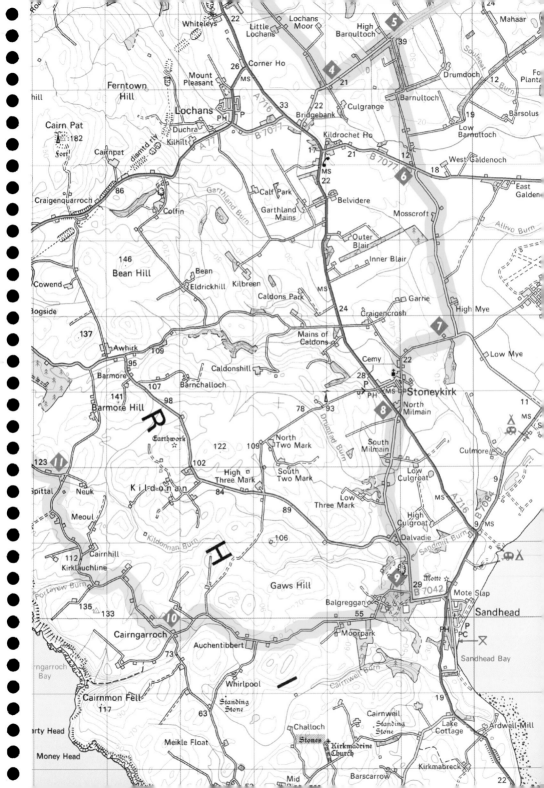

13 Into the Carrick hills and along the River Stinchar east of Girvan

Start

Tourist Information Centre, Girvan, on the west coast south of Ayr

P Long-stay car park next to the Tourist Information Centre

Distance and grade

59 km (37 miles)

Moderate/strenuous

Terrain

Climbs of 149 m (490 ft) south from Girvan at the start and 182 m (600 ft) up over the Carrick Hills out of the Stinchar valley. Highest point – 335 m (1100 ft), 11 km (7 miles) after Barr. Lowest point – sea level at the start

Nearest railway

Girvan

There are two very different faces to Girvan: the main street is full of traffic rumbling through from Stranraer to Ayr along the A77 and holds no great appeal; by contrast, along the seafront there is a wide, attractive promenade (where cycling is permitted) with views across to the island of Ailsa Craig, the outline of Arran and the more distant Mull of Kintyre and Northern Ireland. The harbour is full of fishing boats and yachts. The ride leaves Girvan on an A road carrying two to three cars per minute, which is quite busy by Scottish standards. You climb to almost 152 m (500 ft) before descending to the bridge over the River Stinchar, which you will follow for 16 km (10 miles), passing through the attractive village of Barr where there is a choice of refreshment at one of the two hostelries. The steepest hill starts some 8 km (5 miles) after Barr, climbing 182 m (600 ft) in 4 km (2½ miles). A fast descent through forestry takes you over the Water of Girvan and you are faced with the option of either lengthening your ride by turning north towards Maybole and Dunure or staying on the main route and heading southwest through Dailly to return to Girvan.

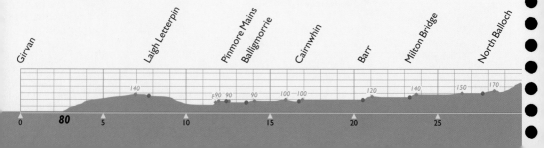

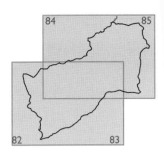

84 | 85

82 | 83

Places of interest

Bargany Gardens 11/12
Azaleas and rhododendrons surround a lily pond in a woodland setting with fine trees, rock garden, walled garden and picnic area

Penkill Castle 11/12 *(just off the route)*
15th-century castle with chesspiece tower, enlarged in 1844 by Spencer Boyd. Pre-Raphaelites painted here

Refreshments

Plenty of choice in **Girvan**
Tea room in **Pinmore**
Kings Arms Hotel, Jolly Shepherd Hotel, **Barr**
Kings Arms Hotel, **Daily**

▼ *Ship repair yards, the harbour, Girvan*

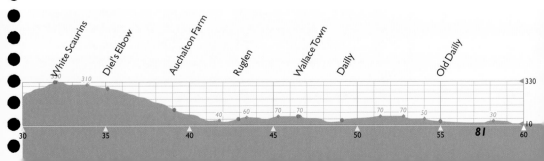

White Scaurins · Diel's Elbow · Auchalton Farm · Ruglen · Wallace Town · Dailly · Old Dailly

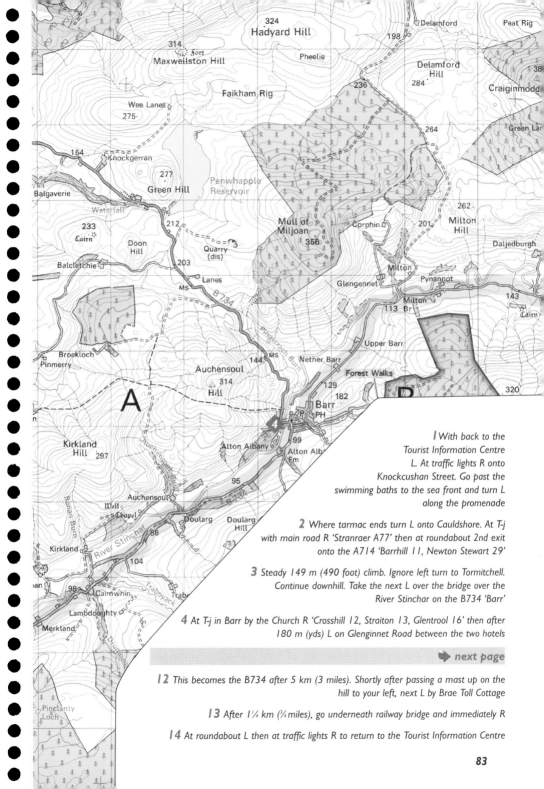

1 With back to the Tourist Information Centre L. At traffic lights R onto Knockcushan Street. Go past the swimming baths to the sea front and turn L along the promenade

2 Where tarmac ends turn L onto Cauldshore. At T-j with main road R 'Stranraer A77' then at roundabout 2nd exit onto the A714 'Barrhill 11, Newton Stewart 29'

3 Steady 149 m (490 foot) climb. Ignore left turn to Tormitchell. Continue downhill. Take the next L over the bridge over the River Stinchar on the B734 'Barr'

4 At T-j in Barr by the Church R 'Crosshill 12, Straiton 13, Glentrool 16' then after 180 m (yds) L on Glenginnet Road between the two hotels

➡ **next page**

12 This becomes the B734 after 5 km (3 miles). Shortly after passing a mast up on the hill to your left, next L by Brae Toll Cottage

13 After 1¼ km (¾ miles), go underneath railway bridge and immediately R

14 At roundabout L then at traffic lights R to return to the Tourist Information Centre

83

4 At T-j in Barr by the church R 'Crosshill 12, Straiton 13, Glentrool 16' then after 180 m (yds) L on Glenginnet Road between the two hotels

5 Follow sings for Newton Stewart. At T-j after 6 km (4 miles) L 'Crosshill, Straiton, Diel's Elbow'

6 Climb hill, then descend through forestry. Emerge from woodland. Ignore a right turn to Straiton 1¼ km (¾ mile) after this turning, and shortly after Auchalton Farm, next L (NS)

7 At T-j with B741 L 'Daily 3, Girvan 9' then after 180 m (yds) 1st R 'Kilkerran Station Yard Public Weighbridge'

8 At T-j shortly after level crossing L 'Girvan 8'.

9 After 3 km (2 miles), cross over the railway bridge. After further 1¼ km (¾ mile) 1st L on the B741 'Dailly, Crosshill, Straiton'

10 On sharp LH bend by the Kings Arms Hotel in Daily continue SA uphill past foodstore

11 At T-j R 'Old Dailly, Girvan, Barr'

◀ previous page

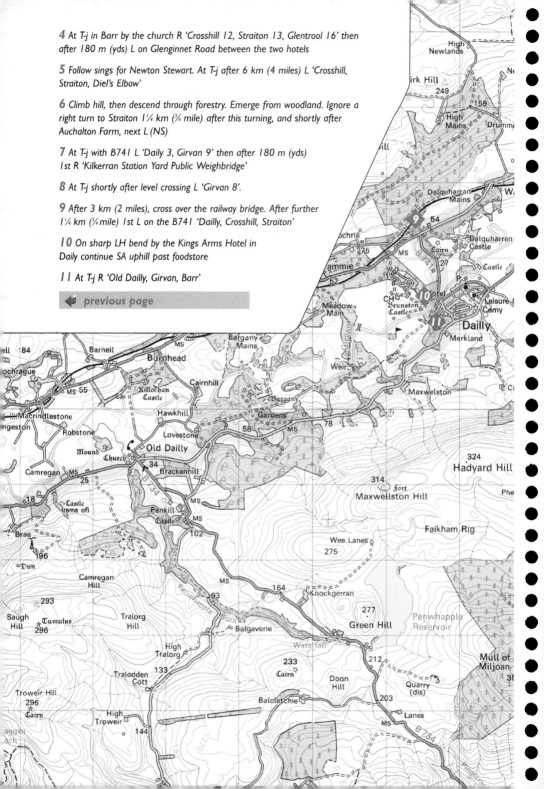

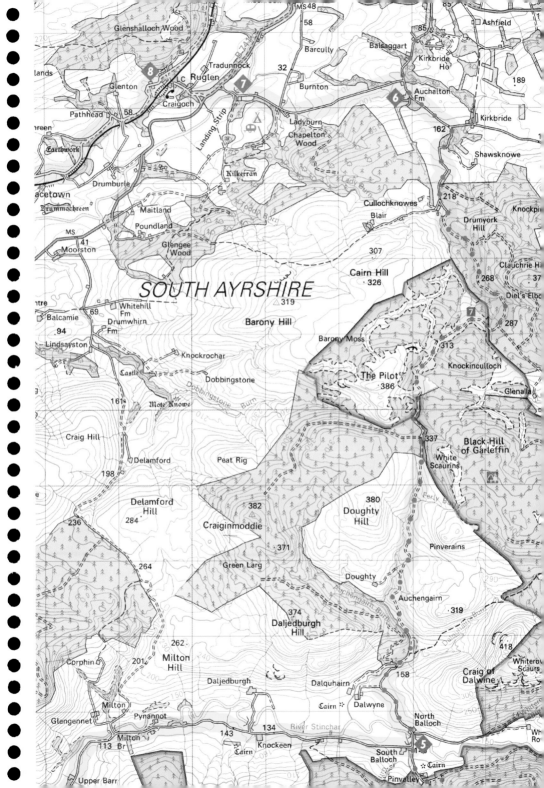

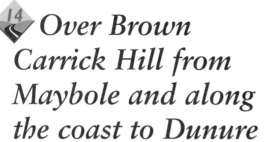

Over Brown Carrick Hill from Maybole and along the coast to Dunure

Start

The Clocktower, high street, Maybole, 16 km (10 miles) south of Ayr

P Follow signs

Distance and grade

43 km (27 miles)

Moderate

Terrain

A 112 m (370 ft) climb from Maybole to the top of Brown Carrick Hill, 131 m (430 ft) climb from Dunure south through Electric Brae and a 146 m (480 ft) climb from Culzean Park over the hills towards Dailly. Highest point – 222 m (730 ft) southeast of Kirkoswald. Lowest point – sea level in Dunure

Nearest railway

Maybole

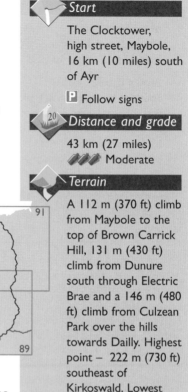

As with Girvan, the main street through Maybole is dominated by traffic on the A77. This is soon left behind as you head north out of the town and steeply up over Brown Carrick Hill. The shape of the hill means that you are suddenly rewarded with the most magnificent views over Ayr Bay and across to the hills of Arran. A fast descent drops you down to the A719, a busier road, but the views across to Arran and the detour to Dunure's picturesque marina and castle ruins more than compensate for the two to three vehicles per minute. Shortly after Culzean Country Park, the route heads inland, over the hills past Kirkoswald towards Dailly. Down in the valley formed by the Water of Girvan, you have a choice of extending the ride via Girvan, Barr and the River Stinchar or opting for the standard route and turning northeast towards Maybole.

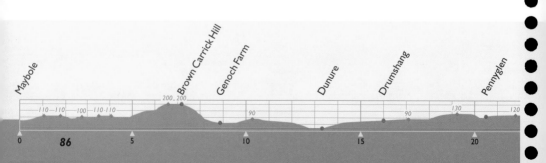

Maybole 1
The restored 17th-century Maybole Castle was the town house of the Kennedy family. The Earls of Cassilis are buried in the 14th-century church, now in ruins

Brown Carrick Hill 3
South of the summit is 1½ km (1 mile) length of road that was given the world's first experimental 'macadam' surface, the predecessor of tarmac, by John Loudon McAdam, the road-maker, who lived at Sauchrie House, halfway up the hill. From the top of the hill there are magnificent views over Ayr Bay, the Firth of Clyde and the peaks of Arran

Dunure 5
The tiny yachting harbour lined with fishermen's cottages and overlooked by the ruined castle where, in 1570, the 4th Earl of Cassilis roasted the Abbot of Crossraguel alive to make him hand over the abbey's lands

Electric Brae 6
An optical illusion that makes the road seem to go uphill when, in fact, it is descending

Culzean Castle 7
The cliff-top mansion was designed by Robert Adam in the 18th century for the 10th Earl of Cassilis. Notable features are the oval staircase and a round drawing room overlooking the Firth of Clyde. The park contains terraced gardens and woodland walks

▲ *Looking towards Arran from Brown Carrick Hill*

Refreshments
*Plenty of choice in **Maybole** Dunure Anchorage PH, tea room, **Dunure***

Morriston Kirkoswald High Newlands Wallacetown Graigfin Wood Drummullan

130 170 70 90 70 70 230

25 30 35 40 **87** 44 20

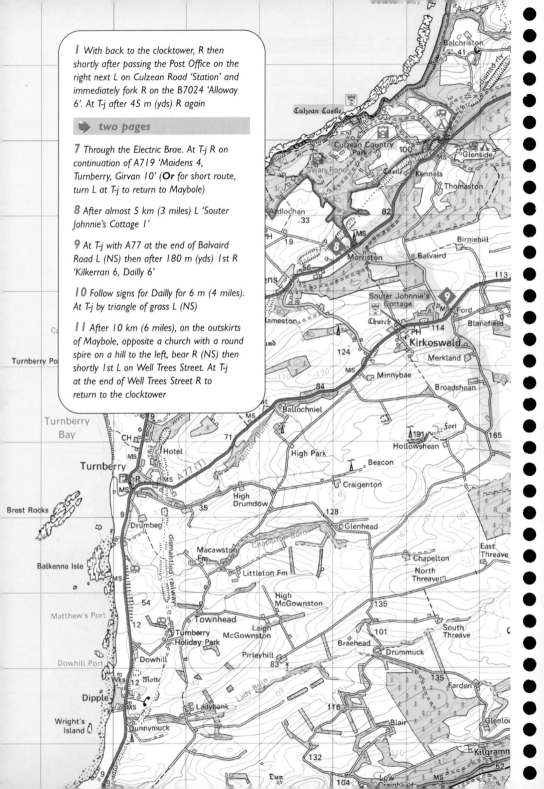

1 With back to the clocktower, R then shortly after passing the Post Office on the right next L on Culzean Road 'Station' and immediately fork R on the B7024 'Alloway 6'. At T-j after 45 m (yds) R again

➡ **two pages**

7 Through the Electric Brae. At T-j R on continuation of A719 'Maidens 4, Turnberry, Girvan 10' (**Or** for short route, turn L at T-j to return to Maybole)

8 After almost 5 km (3 miles) L 'Souter Johnnie's Cottage 1'

9 At T-j with A77 at the end of Balvaird Road L (NS) then after 180 m (yds) 1st R 'Kilkerran 6, Dailly 6'

10 Follow signs for Dailly for 6 m (4 miles). At T-j by triangle of grass L (NS)

11 After 10 km (6 miles), on the outskirts of Maybole, opposite a church with a round spire on a hill to the left, bear R (NS) then shortly 1st L on Well Trees Street. At T-j at the end of Well Trees Street R to return to the clocktower

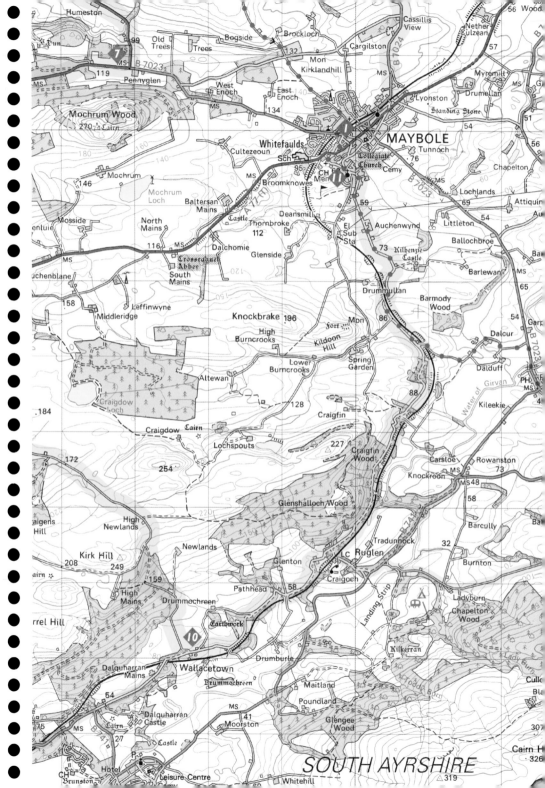

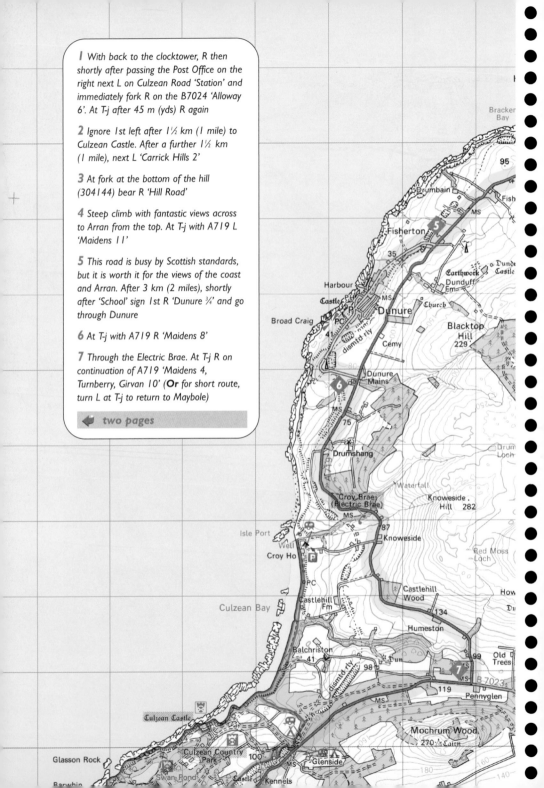

1 With back to the clocktower, R then shortly after passing the Post Office on the right next L on Culzean Road 'Station' and immediately fork R on the B7024 'Alloway 6'. At T-j after 45 m (yds) R again

2 Ignore 1st left after 1½ km (1 mile) to Culzean Castle. After a further 1½ km (1 mile), next L 'Carrick Hills 2'

3 At fork at the bottom of the hill (304144) bear R 'Hill Road'

4 Steep climb with fantastic views across to Arran from the top. At T-j with A719 L 'Maidens 11'

5 This road is busy by Scottish standards, but it is worth it for the views of the coast and Arran. After 3 km (2 miles), shortly after 'School' sign 1st R 'Dunure ¾' and go through Dunure

6 At T-j with A719 R 'Maidens 8'

7 Through the Electric Brae. At T-j R on continuation of A719 'Maidens 4, Turnberry, Girvan 10' (**Or** for short route, turn L at T-j to return to Maybole)

two pages

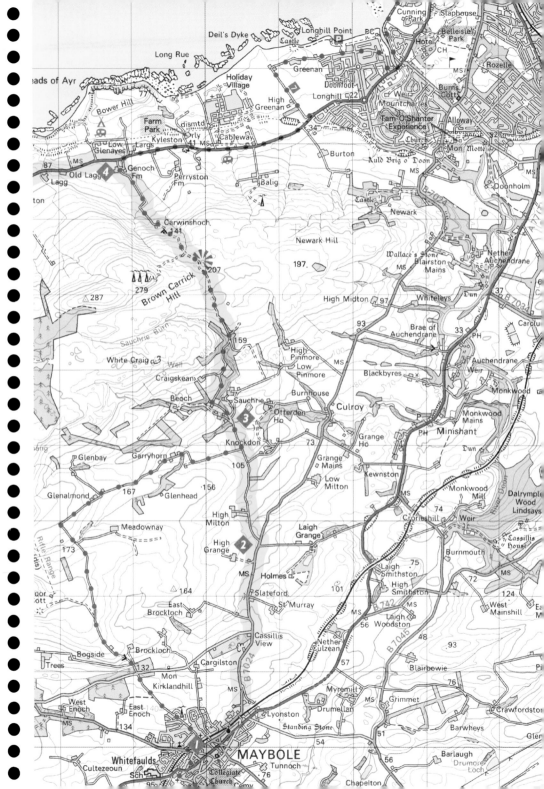

15 *Into old mining country, east of Ayr*

Ayr is on the Sustrans Millennium Route from Carlisle via Dumfries, Gatehouse of Fleet, Maybole and Kilwinning to Glasgow and beyond. The Sustrans route passes along Ayr seafront, which is also the starting point for this ride. Ayr is of sufficient size to generate a high volume of traffic along almost all the approach roads and in the first 13 km (8 miles) of the route you have to cross 5 of them. The linking lanes carry little traffic, particularly the section after the A713 where you feel as though you are in the heart of a rich farming country. There are many views back to the west, over the sea towards Arran. The ride climbs steadily as it heads south, then southwest, dropping briefly into the valley of the River Doon (of *Brigadoon* fame) at Patna, before regaining height on the undulating course back through Dalrymple to Ayr.

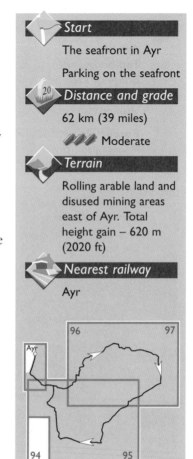

Start
The seafront in Ayr

Parking on the seafront

20 Distance and grade
62 km (39 miles)

/// Moderate

Terrain
Rolling arable land and disused mining areas east of Ayr. Total height gain – 620 m (2020 ft)

Nearest railway
Ayr

Refreshments
Plenty of choice in **Ayr**
Stair Inn, **Stair**
Wheatsheaf Inn, River Doon Hotel, **Patna**
Kirkton Inn,
Dalrymple

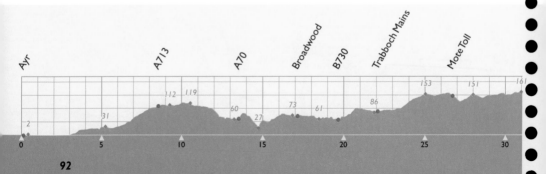

Ayr 1

Two bridges span the River Ayr – the 13th-century Auld Brig and the New Bridge of 1788. Ayr is dominated by the Town Buildings, with their octagonal turret and 38 m (126 ft) steeple. There are Burns, mementos in the Tam o' Shanter Museum

Rozelle House *east of 2*

A Georgian mansion in a 39 ha (96 acre) park. There are woodlands, sculptured gardens, nature trails, a wildfowl pond and local history displays

Alloway *south of 2*

Burns was born here in a thatched cottage in 1759. There is some original furniture. The museum has manuscripts and letters. Close by are the Auld Brig o' Doon and Alloway Kirk, mentioned in the ballad Tam o' Shanter, and the Burns Monument. The Land o' Burns Centre depicts his life and times

▲ Robert Burns Museum, Alloway

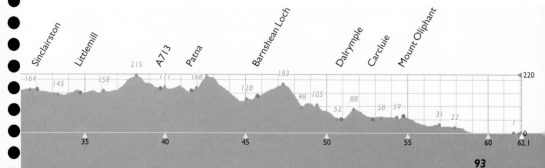

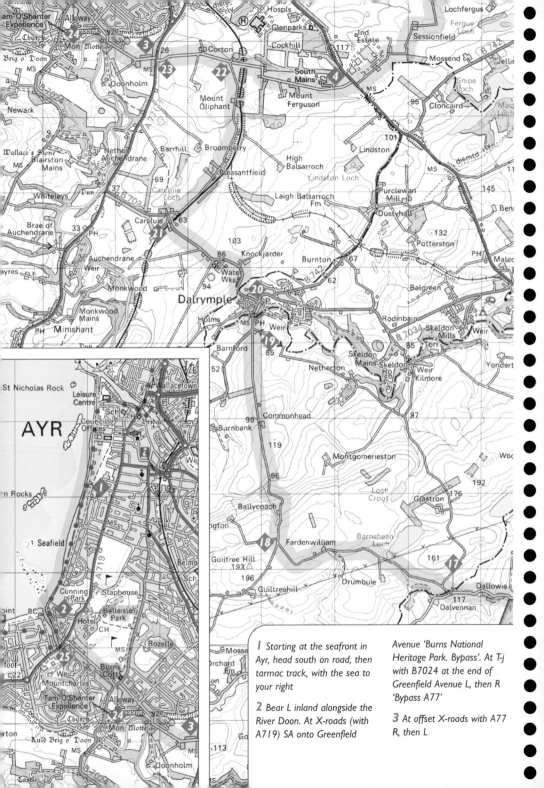

1 Starting at the seafront in Ayr, head south on road, then tarmac track, with the sea to your right

2 Bear L inland alongside the River Doon. At X-roads (with A719) SA onto Greenfield Avenue 'Burns National Heritage Park. Bypass'. At T-j with B7024 at the end of Greenfield Avenue L, then R 'Bypass A77'

3 At offset X-roads with A77 R, then L

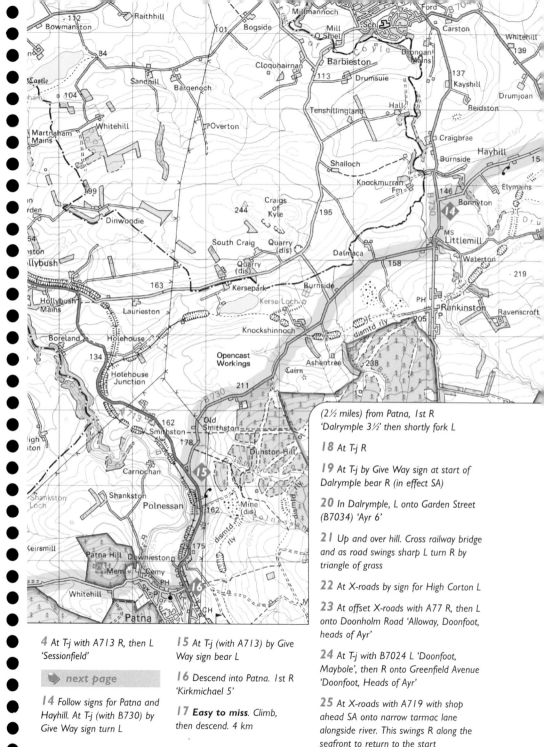

(2½ miles) from Patna, 1st R
'Dalrymple 3½' then shortly fork L

18 At T-j R

19 At T-j by Give Way sign at start of
Dalrymple bear R (in effect SA)

20 In Dalrymple, L onto Garden Street
(B7034) 'Ayr 6'

21 Up and over hill. Cross railway bridge
and as road swings sharp L turn R by
triangle of grass

22 At X-roads by sign for High Corton L

23 At offset X-roads with A77 R, then L
onto Doonholm Road 'Alloway, Doonfoot,
heads of Ayr'

24 At T-j with B7024 L 'Doonfoot,
Maybole', then R onto Greenfield Avenue
'Doonfoot, Heads of Ayr'

25 At X-roads with A719 with shop
ahead SA onto narrow tarmac lane
alongside river. This swings R along the
seafront to return to the start

4 At T-j with A713 R, then L
'Sessionfield'

→ next page

14 Follow signs for Patna and
Hayhill. At T-j (with B730) by
Give Way sign turn L

15 At T-j (with A713) by Give
Way sign bear L

16 Descend into Patna. 1st R
'Kirkmichael 5'

17 **Easy to miss**. Climb,
then descend. 4 km

5 At T-j R, then 1st L

6 **Easy to miss**. Go round sharp bend by farmhouse. 50 m (yd) past next small bungalow on the left turn R through gates sharply back on yourself

7 Through 2nd set of gates. At T-j

with A70 sharply L, then 2nd R (i.e., not Sundrum Castle) onto Uplands Road

8 At T-j R

9 At X-roads with B742 SA 'Stair'

10 At T-j with B730, L for Stair Inn or, for continuation of route, R

'Drongan', then 1st L (NS)

11 At X-roads by Give Way sign SA 'Ochiltree 3'

12 At X-roads SA 'Skares' then shortly, at X-roads with A70, SA 'Skares' (B7046)

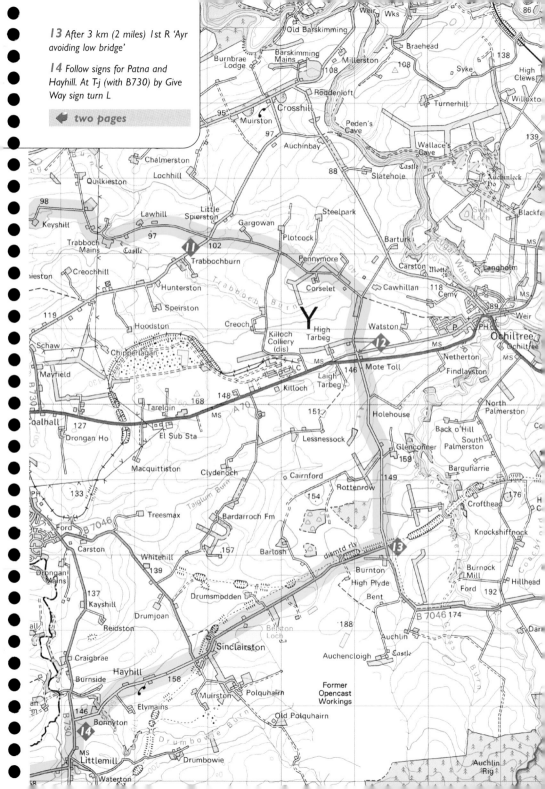

13 After 3 km (2 miles) 1st R 'Ayr avoiding low bridge'

14 Follow signs for Patna and Hayhill. At T-j (with B730) by Give Way sign turn L

← two pages

16 *A circuit of the Isle of Bute*

One of two islands explored off the Ayrshire coast, the Isle of Bute, offers much easier cycling than Arran and with frequent ferry crossings, it is an easy day trip to make. (An even easier, shorter trip could be made from Largs to Great Cumbrae Island where there is a 16 km (10 mile) circuit). One of the most fascinating aspects of cycling on the west coast of Scotland and particularly on the islands is trying to work out the astonishing variety of coastlines, as you complete a full circuit of an island. The cycling is relatively easy with only one climb to note: an ascent near the beginning of 91 m (300 ft) from Kerrycroy Bay through woodland to the high point of the ride where you get your first glimpses of Arran. After this, the ride rarely rises above 45 m (150 ft). In addition to the main circuit described, there are several side trips that can be made: to St Blane's Chapel in the south; to the cafe at Ettrick Bay and north alongside the Kyles of Bute to the ferry quay.

Start

The ferry terminal in Rothesay, Isle of Bute. The ferry to Bute runs from Wemyss Bay (on the A78 between Greenock and Ayr). Caledonian MacBrayne Ferries Head Office, The Ferry Terminal, Gourock. PA19 1QP. Tel: 01745 650100

P At ferry terminal, Wemyss Bay

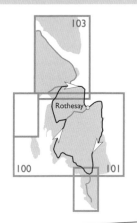

Refreshments

Plenty of choice in **Rothesay**
Kingarth Hotel and tea room
St Blanes Hotel, **Kilchattan Bay**
Ettrick Bay tea room, **Ettrick Bay**

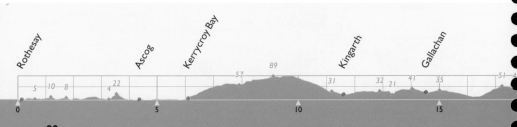

Distance and grade

Basic circuit 35 km
(22 miles) (shorter
circuits also possible).
Side trips: St Blanes
adds 8 km (5 miles).
Ettrick Bay adds 5 km
(3 miles). Rhubodach
adds 19 km (12 miles)

✎ Easy

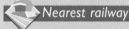

Terrain

Gently rolling country
side with superb views
of other coastlines.
Total height gain –
350 m (1165 ft)

Nearest railway

Wemyss Bay

Places of interest

Rothesay 1

Scottish Kings once came for holidays at the
now ruined Royal Stuart castle which over-
looks this popular resort. There are magnificent floral displays at Ardencraig Gardens

St Blane's Chapel south of 4

Among the remains of the chapel built in
1100 and named after the Celtic saint who
founded the monastery here in AD 575,
there is a fine example of a Norman arch

Viewpoint 5/6

The Highland Boundary Fault formed 400–
600 million years ago when two land masses
moved together causing the rock layers to
buckle and shear. The land to the north rose
– probably higher than the Himalayas are
today – but through time the upper layers
were worn away exposing very old, craggy,
metamorphic rocks

▼ View of the Kyles of Bute

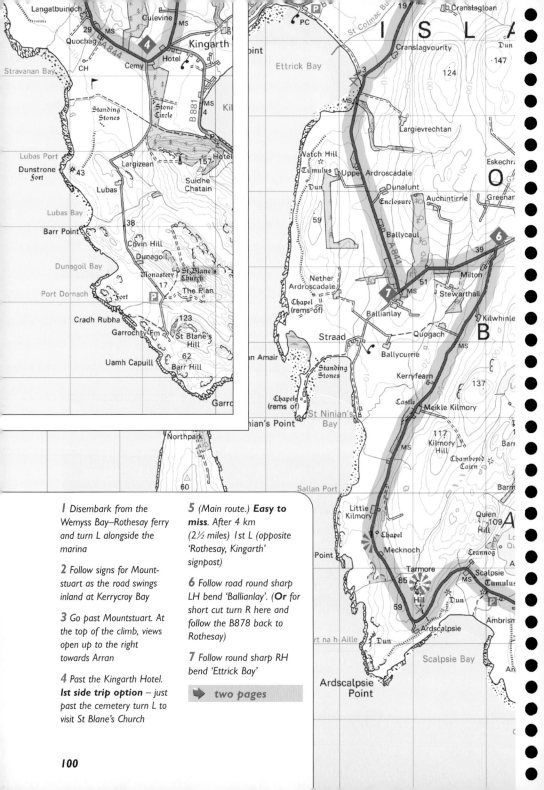

1 Disembark from the Wemyss Bay–Rothesay ferry and turn L alongside the marina

2 Follow signs for Mount-stuart as the road swings inland at Kerrycroy Bay

3 Go past Mountstuart. At the top of the climb, views open up to the right towards Arran

4 Past the Kingarth Hotel. **1st side trip option** – just past the cemetery turn L to visit St Blane's Church

5 (Main route.) **Easy to miss**. After 4 km (2½ miles) 1st L (opposite 'Rothesay, Kingarth' signpost)

6 Follow road round sharp LH bend 'Ballianlay'. (**Or** for short cut turn R here and follow the B878 back to Rothesay)

7 Follow round sharp RH bend 'Ettrick Bay'

➡ **two pages**

8 At T-j R 'Rothesay' (**Or**, for 2nd side trip option, at T-j turn L to visit Ettrick Bay – excellent coffee in the cafe!)

9 At T-j with Kames Bay R 'Port Bannatyne, Rothesay A844'. **3rd side trip option** – at T-j turn L 'Rhubodach' for ferry to Colintraive and fine views of the Kyles of Bute

▼ *View across the moat of Rothesay Castle*

A circuit of the Isle of Arran

The Isle of Arran has been described as Scotland in miniature with lowlands to the south, mountains to the north and a spectacular coastline around its whole circumference. This is a long ride, and although it could be done as a day trip it would be best to take two days and have time to stop and appreciate the views and cafes along the way. If you do decide to complete the circuit in a day, aim either to catch the first ferry in the early morning or the evening ferry at the end of the day (or both). The ride starts by climbing through forestry and down past the golf course. The pattern of the first half of the ride has been established: a climb of 45–110 m (150–350 ft) up from the coast or river valley over the top of the hill and down to the next river or section of coast. A few kilometres north of Blackwaterfoot the road descends to the coast and the long pebble beach is followed for almost 22 km (14 miles) to Lochranza. Beyond lies a long steep climb inland with the crags of the northern massif in dramatic view at the summit. This is followed by a long descent back down to the sea at Sannox Bay and the coastline is followed south to Brodick.

Start

The ferry terminal in Brodick, Isle of Arran.

P At the ferry terminal in Ardrossan, on the A78 between Ayr and Greenock

Distance and grade

Up to 87 km (54 miles)

///// Strenuous

Terrain

Coastline, forestry, arable and pasture land. Wide-ranging views to other coastlines. Total height gain – 950 m (3120 ft)

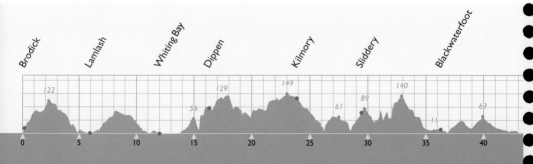

Brodick · Lamlash · Whiting Bay · Dippen · Kilmory · Sliddery · Blackwaterfoot

122 · 129 · 149 · 56 · 61 · 89 · 140 · 11 · 63

0 · 5 · 10 · 15 · 20 · 25 · 30 · 35 · 40

Ferry information

Ardrossan–Brodick.
For ferry times,
contact: Caledonian
MacBrayne Ferries
Head Office, The
Ferry Terminal,
Gourock. PA19 1QP.
Telephone 01745
650100

Nearest railway

Ardrossan

Refreshments

Kingsley PH 🍺, Ormidale PH 🍺,
Brodick
*There are tea rooms, cafes,
hotels and pubs at regular inter-
vals all around the coastline,
even on the northwest coast at
Machrie and Pirnmill. Some of
these are seasonal*

Places of interest

Kildonan 3/4
The area of the 1869–70 gold rush;
prospectors still pan for gold in
Helmsdale's tributaries today. There is a
path to the promontory with views of
rapids and leaping salmon in summer

Kilmory Cairns 3/4
Torrylin, a Neolithic chambered cairn, lies
southwest of Kilmory village. Skeletal
remains and a flint knife were found here

Blackwaterfoot 5
A hamlet standing amid ancient remains.
Robert Bruce may have sheltered to the
north of the settlement at King's Cave in
the 14th century

Machrie Moor 6
The remains of six four metre (15 ft)
Bronze Age stone circles lie scattered
within a kilometre (¾ mile), south of
Machrie. Nearby are traces of Stone Age
hut circles and tombs

Brodick Castle and Country Park *near
to the end, 3 km (2 miles) from Brodick 8*
The seat of the Dukes of Hamilton, built
in the 13th century with later additions.
The interior features fine plaster ceilings,
furniture, porcelain and paintings. The
grounds include a 1710 formal garden, a
Victorian rose garden and a nature trail

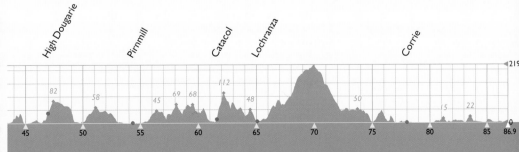

▲ *Goat Fell and Brodick Bay*

1 Disembark from ferry in Brodick, turn L 'South' (**Or** for shorter, northern loop turn R and follow signs for 'West. B880, Blackwaterfoot', then turn R on A841 and continue from instruction point 5)

2 Climb, then descend into Lamlash

3 For **1st short cut** and off-road option – at the end of Lamlash on sharp LH bend 1st proper road R 'Sliddery via Ross 8' then, for off-road section, soon after Dyemill

Chalets to the left turn L by Forest Enterprise signboard 'Forest Walks to Lagaville, Urie Loch, Whiting Bay and Kilmory'. Follow signs for Kilmory

4 On main route – pass through Whiting Bay, turn west, drop into then climb out of Lagg. (**Or** – for **2nd short cut** – over 1 km (¾ mile) after Lagg turn R by chapel on minor road to return to Lamlash)

5 For **3rd short cut** – 11 km (7 miles) after Lagg, on sharp LH bend on flat section just before

Blackwaterfoot, bear R (in effect SA) (NS). Follow the B880 back to Brodick

6 For **4th and final short cut option** – 8 km (5 miles) north of Blackwaterfoot turn R in Machrie Bay to join B880 and return to Brodick

7 Long flat coastal section with views across to the Mull of Kintyre

8 Longest, steepest climb of the ride southeast from Lochranza 200 m (660 ft)

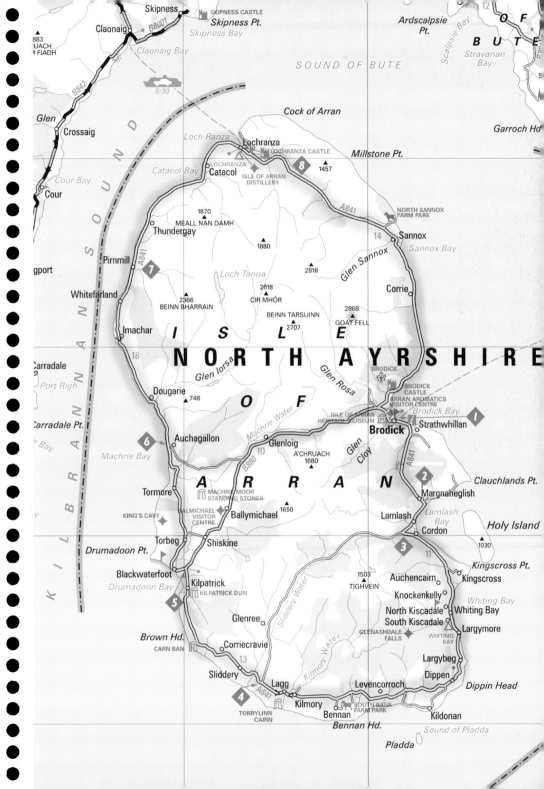

Railway paths between Lochwinnoch and Greenock

Lochwinnoch is the scenic start to this route on the banks of Castle Semple Loch, where there is immediate access onto the first of two good-quality railway paths. There are many options for the train to take you to the start or bring you back from the end of this bike ride. The railway paths link at Johnstone where there is a magnificent metal sculpture marking the junction. The route into Glasgow, following the right-hand fork, is fragmented using a mixture of roads, streets, parks, railway lines and riverside paths. The left-hand fork continues through Bridge of Weir and Kilmacolm climbing to the high point of the route at over 120 m (400 ft). The route above Port Glasgow is broken in several places by street sections, but on a fine day the views of the busy docks and shipping activity against a backdrop of Scottish mountains are so dramatic that it is worth continuing to the path's end at Greenock.

 Start

The Castle Semple Visitor Centre, Lochwinnoch, 26 km (16 miles) west of Glasgow on the A760

P As above

 Distance and grade

58 km (36 miles). This is a linear, there-and-back route so you can easily shorten the ride

Easy

 Terrain

Dismantled railway path through woodland and above the Clyde Estuary. Gentle climb to high point of 130 m (423 ft) between Kilmacolm and Port Glasgow

Nearest railway

Lochwinnoch (at the south end); Johnstone; Port Glasgow and Greenock (best to use Whinhill Station)

 Lochwinnoch

Low Semple

 Kilbarchan

Johnstone

54

39

0

5

10

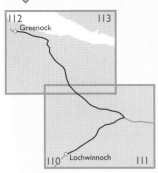

Lochwinnoch 1
Colour-washed houses date from the early 19th century. The village was a centre of the cask and barrel-making industry. There is sailing and canoeing on the loch in Castle Semple Country Park

Kilmacolm 6
The village grew from a small rural hamlet founded in the 7th or 8th century and takes its name from the Church of Columba. The railway arrived in 1869 and many of Scotland's finest architects of the period, including Mackintosh and Salmon, were commissioned to build grand homes. As a result, part of the village is a conservation area

Quarriers Village 6/7
This unique conservation village was built by William Quarrier in the last quarter of the 19th century to provide homes for orphans. Today many of the stone villas are in private ownership and some of the communal buildings now house a craft centre and restaurant

Greenock 12
The Inverclyde town famous for ships and sugar is also the birthplace of James Watt, improver of the steam engine. The Comet, Britain's first passenger steamboat, was built at nearby Port Glasgow in 1812. A replica is on show at near Port Glasgow Railway Station

Refreshments

Mossend PH 🍺, plenty of choice in **Lochwinnoch**
Plenty of choice in **Bridge of Weir**
Plenty of choice in **Kilmacolm**

▲ *The railway path between Lochwinnoch and Johnstone*

1 From the Castle Semple Visitor Centre in Lochwinnoch, exit car park and just before bridge turn sharp R uphill onto cycle track

2 Go past Castle Semple Loch and temple ruins to the right

3 Shortly after the houses start on the outskirts of Johnstone the track runs parallel to, then crosses dual carriageway (A737 Johnstone bypass)

4 Cross the B789 via pelican crossing following signs for Paisley

5 At large pointed sculpture (Aurora Borealis - Sentinel) turn L to cross bridge over dual

carriageway and head west towards Greenock (**Or** turn R here for Paisley and Glasgow - the route is way-marked but soon becomes

fragmented using a mixture of roads, pavements and parks)

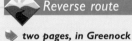 **two pages**

Reverse route

 two pages, in Greenock

H Follow fine gravel path for 11 km (7 miles). At T-j immediately after bridge over dual carriageway by amazing metal sculpture turn R for Lochwinnoch or L for Paisley and Glasgow

I Cross B789 via pelican crossing, then after 1 km (¾ mile) bear R uphill onto tarmac track to cross bridge over dual carriageway (A737)

J Follow for 8 km (5 miles), passing alongside Castle Semple Loch, keeping an eye out for Castle Semple Visitor Centre down to your right

6 *Follow railway path for 11 km (7 miles), passing through Bridge of Weir. At the Pullman PH at Kilmacolm bear R, then L past the pub, through small metal arch. At T-j in housing estate, turn R then shortly rejoin cycle path*

7 *At fork of tracks by barrier and signboard shortly after passing beneath two sets of pylons turn L uphill*

8 *At T-j with road with modern houses ahead turn L (near Milton Road)*

9 *At T-j with Dubbs Road at the end of Montrose Avenue go SA across grassy strip onto road by houses. Turn L, then R. At T-j with Crosshill Road SA onto continuation of cycle path*

10 *At X-roads with busy, steep road SA*

11 *The track zigzags down steeply. Superb views of the Clyde. Shortly after crossing long metal and wooden bridge across gully turn sharply L uphill*

12 *The track ends near to Lady Octavia Recreation Centre on Bridgend Road at the eastern end of Greenock*

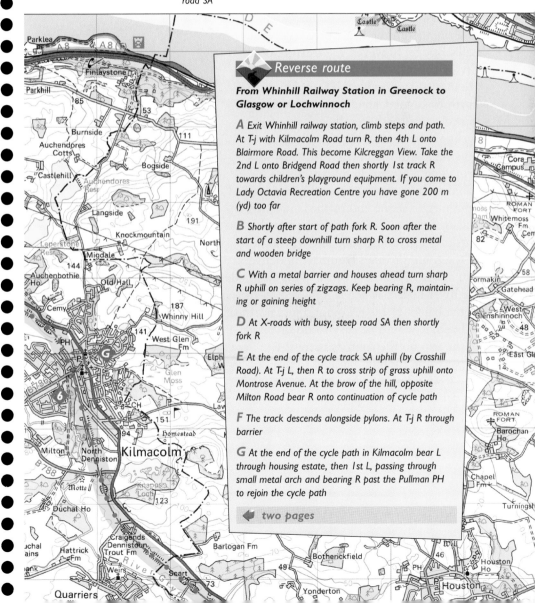

◀ two pages

Reverse route

From Whinhill Railway Station in Greenock to Glasgow or Lochwinnoch

A *Exit Whinhill railway station, climb steps and path. At T-j with Kilmacolm Road turn R, then 4th L onto Blairmore Road. This become Kilcreggan View. Take the 2nd L onto Bridgend Road then shortly 1st track R towards children's playground equipment. If you come to Lady Octavia Recreation Centre you have gone 200 m (yd) too far*

B *Shortly after start of path fork R. Soon after the start of a steep downhill turn sharp R to cross metal and wooden bridge*

C *With a metal barrier and houses ahead turn sharp R uphill on series of zigzags. Keep bearing R, maintaining or gaining height*

D *At X-roads with busy, steep road SA then shortly fork R*

E *At the end of the cycle track SA uphill (by Crosshill Road). At T-j L, then R to cross strip of grass uphill onto Montrose Avenue. At the brow of the hill, opposite Milton Road bear R onto continuation of cycle path*

F *The track descends alongside pylons. At T-j R through barrier*

G *At the end of the cycle path in Kilmacolm bear L through housing estate, then 1st L, passing through small metal arch and bearing R past the Pullman PH to rejoin the cycle path*

◀ two pages

2 From Clydebank to the banks of Loch Lomond

This route uses a scenic stretch of the Sustrans Millennium Route that will, upon completion, run all the way from Dover to Inverness. It would be possible to start this ride right from the heart of Glasgow at Bell's Bridge; however, the starting point at Clydebank has been chosen so that you are immediately onto the towpath of the Forth & Clyde Canal, a broad, well-maintained gravel path, totally suitable for cycling. The canal links the Clyde at Bowling, with the Forth near to Falkirk providing many cycling possibilities, avoiding busy roads between Glasgow and Edinburgh. At the end of the canal section, a dismantled railway is followed to the outskirts of Dumbarton. The waymarking of the route through Dumbarton delivers you safely to the start of the path alongside the River Leven, which is followed all the way to the banks of Loch Lomond just north of Balloch. It would be easy to do one half of the trip on the train as there is a railway line running parallel to the ride from Glasgow, through Clydebank to Balloch.

Start
Clydebank Railway Station, west of Glasgow/the Playdrome Shopping Centre, Clydebank

P The Playdrome car park, Clydebank

Distance
43 km (27 miles). This is a linear, there-and-back route so you can easily shorten the ride

Easy

Terrain
Canal towpath, dismantled railway path and riverside path. Fine loch views. No climbs

Nearest railway
Clydebank, Dumbarton, Balloch

Refreshments
Plenty of choice in **Clydebank, Dumbarton** and **Balloch**

Clydebank   Mountblow   Erskine Bridge   Bowling   Milton

12   9   12   5   10

0   5   10

History of the Cycleway
Opened in 1989, the Glasgow to Loch Lomond Cycleway was the first long-distance cycleway in the West of Scotland. It starts from Bell's Bridge near the Conference Centre, which is also the junction of other major long distance cycle routes: Glasgow to Greenock, Glasgow to Ardrossan (see off-road Route 1) and the planned Glasgow to Edinburgh route. The Loch Lomond route (off-road Route 2) runs parallel to the River Clyde along the old railway line from Partick through Whiteinch and Yoker to Clydebank

Erskine Bridge 1/2
Opened in 1971, the box-girder bridge has a main span of 310 m (1000 ft) and a total length of 1320 m (4334 ft) and was designed to withstand winds of 210 kph (130 mph). Its deck stands 55 m (180 ft) above the river thus allowing large ships to sail underneath and on to destinations further up the Clyde

Clydebank District Museum 1
The great ships the Queen Mary, Queen Elizabeth and Queen Elizabeth II were built at the famous John Brown's shipyard in the centre of Clydebank. Brown's was only one of several great shipyards with a long tradition of ship-building in Clydebank and the museum has a fine collection of models of many of the ships built here

Dumbarton 3
The viewpoint of Dumbarton Rock, overlooking the mouth of the River Leven, is where the fortress-capital of the Kingdom of Strathclyde was established about 1500 years ago. A much later castle is maintained as an ancient monument. In the heart of the town itself is the fascinating industrial museum known as the Denny Experiment Tank. This is where Dennys of Dumbarton, who were also pioneers in helicopter, hydrofoil and hovercraft design, used to test scale models of their latest ships, in a 100 m (330 ft) channel simulating stormy seas

▲ *Along the railway path between Lochwinnoch and Johnstone*

Dennystown

Renton

Jamestown

Balloch

3 5   1 3 6   7

43

15   20   22.2

0

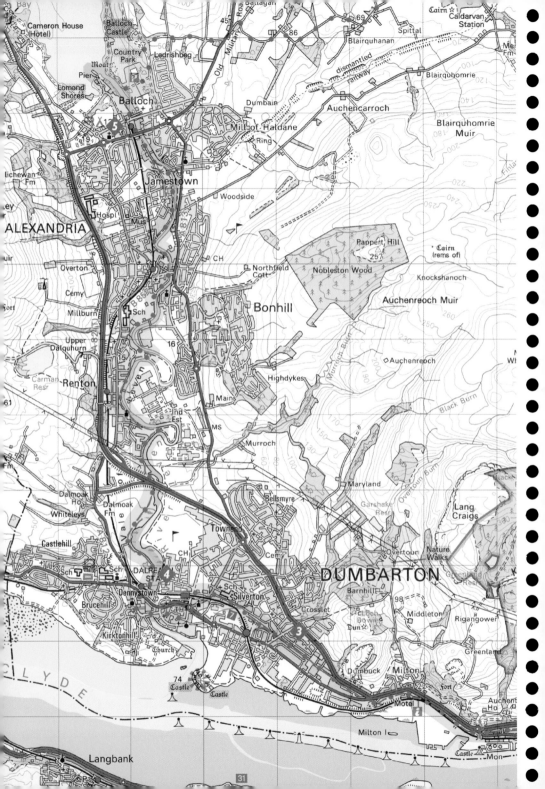

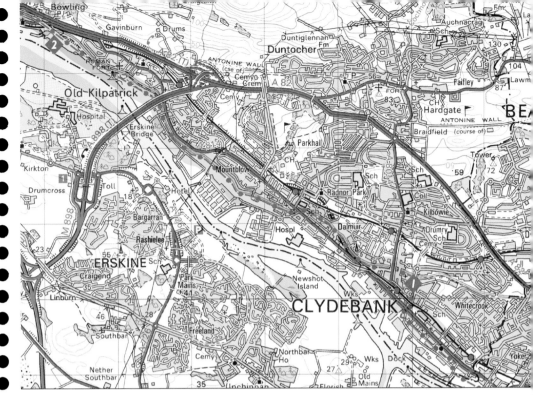

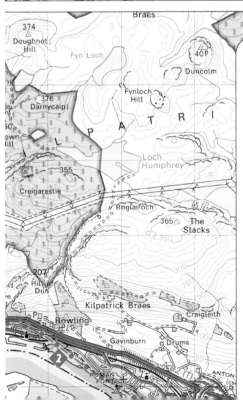

1 *From the Playdrome Shopping Centre in Clydebank (**Or** Clydebank railway station) join the Forth and Clyde Canal towpath heading west towards Dumbarton and Loch Lomond*

2 *After 8 km (5 miles), at a large metal bridge over the canal by a bike hire outlet and small marina turn R uphill, cross road, then turn L*

3 *Railway path section through woodland and exposed rocks. At the end of cycle path at T-j with Third Avenue on the outskirts of Dumbarton turn L and follow excellent signposting through Dumbarton to the banks of the River Leven. If you get lost, ask for Dumbarton Central Railway Station and pick up the path from there*

4 *Rejoin cyclepath along the banks of River Leven and follow for 10 km (6 miles) to Balloch*

5 *At the marina in Balloch turn L towards the Tourist Information Centre, then R onto gravel track to continue to the shores of Loch Lomond. Retrace route*

3 *From Aberfoyle to Callander*

Aberfoyle is at the heart of the Queen Elizabeth Forest Park and there are several waymarked forestry routes in the three sections of forestry near the town. This ride uses the green waymarked forestry route through Achray Forest that starts at the east end of the village of Aberfoyle near the golf course, climbing parallel with the road over Duke's Pass, dropping past Loch Drunkie, then turning sharp right and eastwards along the shores of Loch Venachar. It is worth forming a clear picture of the various junctions in the forestry on your outward route so that you do not miss them on your way back. The ride alongside Loch Venachar is a very lovely stretch with views of Ben Ledi across the water. Callander is a handsome tourist town at the start of the Highlands. As this is a there-and-back route it can easily be shortened and it is just as easily started from Callander.

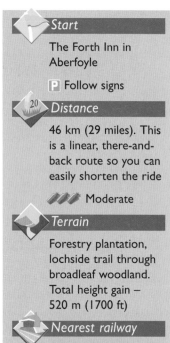

Start

The Forth Inn in Aberfoyle

P Follow signs

Distance

46 km (29 miles). This is a linear, there-and-back route so you can easily shorten the ride

/// Moderate

Terrain

Forestry plantation, lochside trail through broadleaf woodland. Total height gain – 520 m (1700 ft)

Nearest railway

Dunblane, 19 km (12 miles) southeast of Callander

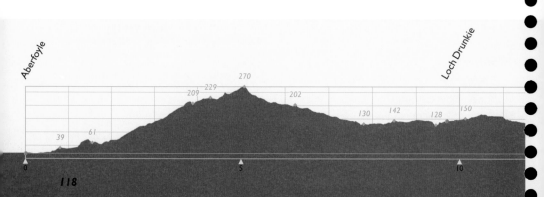

Aberfoyle 1

Traditionally marks the boundary between the Scottish Lowlands and Highlands. The village expanded when the Duke's Road was built in 1820 for the Duke of Montrose to give easier access to the Trossachs. This 8 km (5 mile) wide strip of birch-covered mountains, rocky crags, streams and moorland was the setting for Sir Walter Scott's novel *Rob Roy* and his poem *Lady of the Lake*. The slate quarries on Mentieth Hill behind the village were worked for almost 200 years, producing up to a million and a half roofing slates a year, before closing in the 1950s. North of the village is the Queen Elizabeth Forest Park Visitor Centre

Blackwater Marshes 8

A site of special scientific interest with reeds, willow and birch trees, and patches of bog myrtle. The home of a variety of wildfowl including grey lag geese, goosanders, teal and wigeon. The open territory is excellent for birds of prey. Nesting boxes have been put up to encourage barn owls

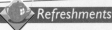

Refreshments

Plenty of choice in **Aberfoyle**
Byre Inn 🍴🍴, **Brig o' Turk**
(just north of the route at instruction 8)
Plenty of choice in
Callander

▲ *Loch Venachar and the Trossachs*

West Dullater   Gartchonzie   Callander

271

92 92 88   88   104 89   91 91   94   94   81   69   69

19

15   20   23.0

Take care not to mistake the faded yellow line of the national park boundary for the solid yellow line of the route

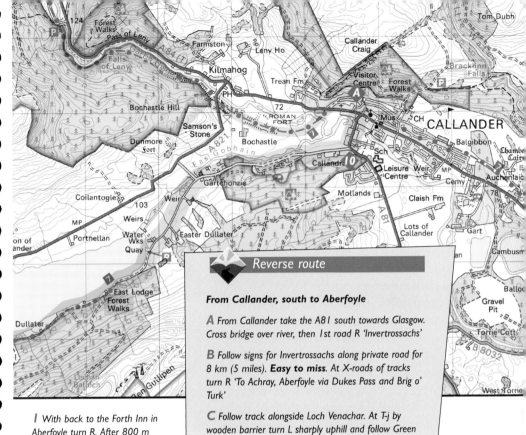

Reverse route

From Callander, south to Aberfoyle

A From Callander take the A81 south towards Glasgow. Cross bridge over river, then 1st road R 'Invertrossachs'

B Follow signs for Invertrossachs along private road for 8 km (5 miles). **Easy to miss**. At X-roads of tracks turn R 'To Achray, Aberfoyle via Dukes Pass and Brig o' Turk'

C Follow track alongside Loch Venachar. At T-j by wooden barrier turn L sharply uphill and follow Green Bike Ride signs past Loch Drunkie back towards Aberfoyle

D Just before the golf course in Aberfoyle turn sharp R downhill to join the A821

1 With back to the Forth Inn in Aberfoyle turn R. After 800 m (½ mile), shortly after children's playground on the right, turn L immediately before end of speed limit signs 'Dounay Centre'

2 Follow through car park bearing R uphill past the golf course. At T-j with forestry track turn sharp L 'Trossachs, Green Bike Route'

3 Follow Green Bike Route signs. Climb steadily for 1 km (¾ mile). At T-j sharp L

4 At X-roads SA. Climb alongside stream, then shortly 1st L away from stream continuing to climb

5 At X-roads with Forest Drive by wooden barrier and 'Achray Forest Drive' sign go SA 'Trossachs' then shortly 2nd L, leaving the Forest Drive

6 Rejoin the Forest Drive, bearing L by Loch Drunkie. Follow the edge of the loch

7 At fork, soon after the car park on the right, bear R 'Green/Blue Bike Routes'

8 **Easy to miss**. Near the bottom of fast descent turn R sharply back on yourself by yellow and brown wooden barrier 'To Callander via Loch Venachar'. (If you come to a wide, open marsh area to the right with a 'Blachwater Marshes' signboard you have gone too far and should retrace)

9 The track runs alongside the edge of Loch Venachar. At X-roads with tarmac lane turn L

10 Follow lane for 8 km (5 miles). At T-j with A81 L into Callander.

From Callander to the banks of Loch Voil

Starting from Callander, the ride described here soon leaves the main road and drops down onto the course of the old Caledonian Railway line to Oban, which was closed in 1965. There is a delightful woodland section alongside the Falls of Leny with views of Ben Ledi opening up ahead, a peak that can easily be climbed on a path starting near the forest cabins and car park on the west side of the river. The route follows the west bank of Loch Lubnaig, climbing away from the dismantled railway on more than one occasion to join the waymarked forestry tracks. Beyond Strathyre, the route continues on quiet lanes to Balquhidder, the location of Rob Roy's grave. You can extend the ride along the banks of Loch Voil as far as the Monachyle Mhor Hotel or further, to Inverlochlarig, the site of Rob Roy's house.

Start

Tourist Information Centre, Callander, on the A84 between Stirling and Crianlarich

P Follow signs

Distance and grade

46 km (29 miles). This is a linear, there-and-back route so you can easily shorten the ride

Easy

Terrain

Dismantled railway through wooded valley, forestry, minor lanes, loch views. Total height gain – 370 m (1215 ft)

Nearest railway

Dunblane, 19 km (12 miles) southeast of Callander

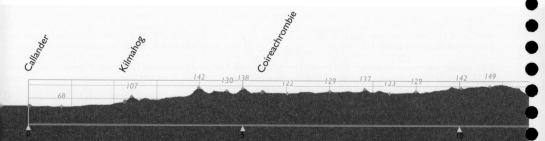

Callander — 68

Kilmahog — 107

142 130 138 Coireachrombie

122 129 137 123 129 142 149

0   5   10

Callander 1

18th-century houses line Ancaster Square. In Victorian times, the Caledonian Railway Company took advantage of easy gradients to work their rail route from Callander to Oban via Crianlarich. With the Callander–Crianlarich section closing in 1965 the track bed now provides an ideal cycle route into the hills

Pass of Leny 4

The dramatic Pass of Leny has been one of the main routes to and from the Highlands for thousands of years. Close to Kilmahog an ancient iron age fort guards the entrance to the pass. Today the greatest spectacle is the raging falls, an impressive sight after heavy rain

▲ *Descending towards Loch Lubnaig*

Balquhidder 11

Loch Voil is rich in salmon and trout and all around are the Braes of Balquhidder, the steep glens and windswept hills framed by mountain peaks to the northwest. Rob Roy MacGregor died near the village in 1734 and is buried in the churchyard. Although the MacGregors ruled the district at that time, Balquhidder and its surroundings were originally the domain of the Maclarens; there is a monument in the churchyard commemorating stirring chapters in the clan's history

Refreshments

Plenty of choice in **Callander**
Plenty of choice in **Strathyre**
Stronvar tea rooms, just south of **Balquhidder** *(open March-October)*
Monachyle Hotel, **Loch Voil**

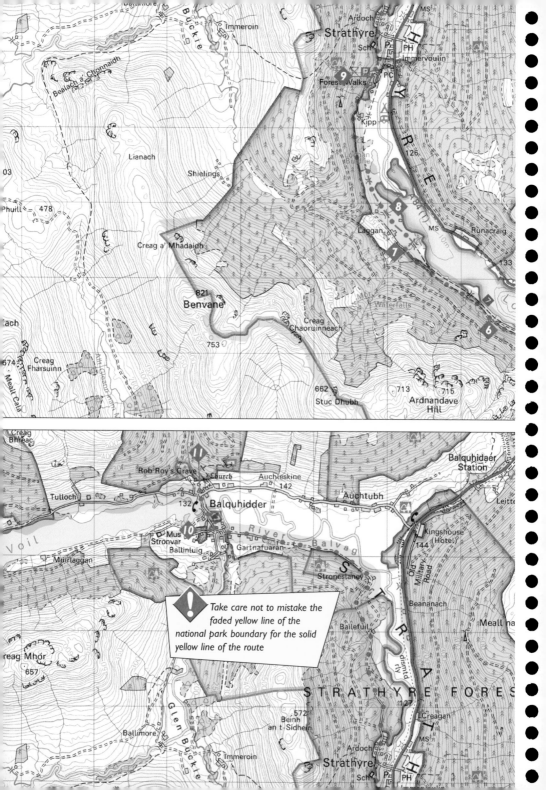

Take care not to mistake the faded yellow line of the national park boundary for the solid yellow line of the route

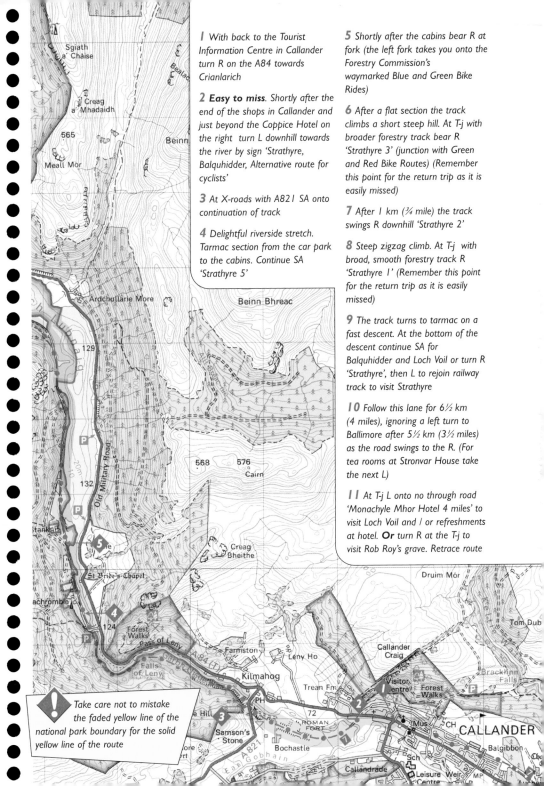

1 With back to the Tourist Information Centre in Callander turn R on the A84 towards Crianlarich

2 **Easy to miss**. Shortly after the end of the shops in Callander and just beyond the Coppice Hotel on the right turn L downhill towards the river by sign 'Strathyre, Balquhidder, Alternative route for cyclists'

3 At X-roads with A821 SA onto continuation of track

4 Delightful riverside stretch. Tarmac section from the car park to the cabins. Continue SA 'Strathyre 5'

5 Shortly after the cabins bear R at fork (the left fork takes you onto the Forestry Commission's waymarked Blue and Green Bike Rides)

6 After a flat section the track climbs a short steep hill. At T-j with broader forestry track bear R 'Strathyre 3' (junction with Green and Red Bike Routes) (Remember this point for the return trip as it is easily missed)

7 After 1 km (¾ mile) the track swings R downhill 'Strathyre 2'

8 Steep zigzag climb. At T-j with broad, smooth forestry track R 'Strathyre 1' (Remember this point for the return trip as it is easily missed)

9 The track turns to tarmac on a fast descent. At the bottom of the descent continue SA for Balquhidder and Loch Voil or turn R 'Strathyre', then L to rejoin railway track to visit Strathyre

10 Follow this lane for 6½ km (4 miles), ignoring a left turn to Ballimore after 5½ km (3½ miles) as the road swings to the R. (For tea rooms at Stronvar House take the next L)

11 At T-j L onto no through road 'Monachyle Mhor Hotel 4 miles' to visit Loch Voil and / or refreshments at hotel. **Or** turn R at the T-j to visit Rob Roy's grave. Retrace route

Take care not to mistake the faded yellow line of the national park boundary for the solid yellow line of the route

Notes

Notes

Useful addresses

British Cycling Federation
National Cycling Centre
Stuart Street
Manchester M11 4DQ
0870 871 2000
www.bcf.uk.com

The BCF co-ordinates and promotes an array of cycle sports and cycling in general. They are a good first point of contact if you want to find out more about how to get involved in cycling. The website provides information on upcoming cycle events and competitions.

CTC (Cyclists Touring Club)
Cotterell House
69 Meadrow
Godalming
Surrey GU7 3HS
01483 417217
www.ctc.org.uk

Britain's largest cycling organisation, promoting recreational and utility cycling. The CTC provides touring and technical advice, legal aid and insurance, and campaigns to improve facilities and opportunities for all cyclists. The website provides details of campaigns and routes and has an online application form.

The London Cycling Campaign
Unit 228
30 Great Guildford Street
London SE1 0HS
020 7928 7220
www.lcc.org.uk

The LCC promotes cycling in London by providing services for cyclists and by campaigning for more facilities for cyclists. Membership of the LCC provides the following benefits: London Cyclist magazine, insurance, legal advice, workshops, organised rides, discounts in bike shops and much more. You can join the LCC on its website.

Sustrans
Head Office
Crown House
37-41 Prince Street
Bristol BS1 4PS
General information line: 0117 929 0888
www.sustrans.org.uk

A registered charity, Sustrans designs and builds systems for sustainable transport. It is best known for its transformation of old railway lines into safe, traffic-free routes for cyclists and pedestrians and wheelchair users. Sustrans is developing the 13,000 km (8000 mile) National Cycle Network on traffic-calmed minor roads and traffic-free paths, to be completed by the year 2005 with major funding from the Millennium Commission.

Veteran Cycle Club
Membership Secretary
31 Yorke Road
Croxley Green
Rickmansworth
Herts WD3 3DW
www.v-cc.org.uk

A very active club, the VCC is concerned with the history and restoration of veteran cycles. Members enjoy organised rides and receive excellent publications relating to cycle history and club news.